# R&D *Essays on the Economics of Research and Development*

**RANDOM HOUSE**

*New York*

# R&D

## Essays on the Economics of Research and Development

*by* DANIEL HAMBERG

*State University of New York at Buffalo*

*A portion of Chapter 5 appeared in
the Journal of Political Economy,
April, 1963. Copyright 1963 by
the University of Chicago.*

*Manufactured in the United States of America
by H. Wolff Book Manufacturing Co., New York*

*To Eva,* *who gave birth to my wife*

# Preface

Work on this collection of essays had its inception as far back as 1959, when I was asked by the Joint Economic Committee of the Congress to prepare testimony for its Hearings on Employment, Growth, and Price Levels. The result was a paper entitled "Size of Firm, Monopoly, and Economic Growth," which dealt with the relationship between company size and industry concentration on the one hand and invention and innovation on the other. The investigations for this paper stirred my interest in a comparatively new subject, the economics of research and development, to the point where that study led to another, and then another, and so on. The results of this series of studies comprise, more or less, the contents of this book.

The greater part of this book reflects the orientation of the initial work, but, after pondering the subject at some length, I wrote another chapter on the results of a rather large-scale statistical analysis of the determinants of research and development in industry.

It is not unnatural for an economist working on this subject to begin to wonder also about optimizing the allocation of a research and development budget. The final chapter, which brings together these thoughts, describes a linear-programming model for selecting and evaluating an optimum set of research and development projects.

Much of the materials in all but the last two chapters have been published before and are being republished here because they seem to have stirred a great deal of interest. Requests from a variety of sources for copies of the originally published papers have exceeded their supply, and this book seemed a good way of making them generally available. However, all have been updated and carefully edited in the process of incorporating them into the book. Along these lines, I have included only parts of the Joint Economic Committee paper referred to above, because this paper has been reprinted more than once in volumes edited by others.

I wish to take this opportunity to express my thanks to a number of colleagues. Among these are Professors Nanda K. Choudhry, now of the University of Toronto, and Rubin Saposnik, of the University of Buffalo, who rendered advice and assistance unstintingly when asked. The members of the Seminar on Law and Technology, sponsored by the University of Wisconsin Law School under the auspices of the Ford Foundation, provided many helpful comments in the course of the development of Chapter 5; I wish to thank, especially, Professors Jacob Schmookler, Robert Merrill, John Stedman, Harrison White, and John Heath. Very much more than the usual debt of gratitude must also be expressed to my friend, John Buehler, a former graduate student at the University of Buffalo and now a member of the faculty of Florida State University; the amount of work that he put into Chapter 6 makes him a virtual coauthor of that essay. I am also grateful to Professor Otto Eckstein of Harvard who, as Director of the Study of Employment, Growth, and Price Levels, started me on this research.

For financial assistance at various stages of the work included in this volume, I am indebted to the Ford Foundation, the Research Foundation of the State University of New York, the University of Buffalo, and the University of Maryland. Gratitude is also due the Computer Center of the University of Buffalo for its splendid services.

Finally, I wish to thank *Challenge, the Magazine of Economic Affairs* (Haig Babian, Editor), a publication of Challenge Communications, Inc., for permission to use material from the following articles of mine first published there:

"Less Noise, More Research," May 1961, pp. 16-20.

"Our Antiquated' Patent System," January 1962, pp. 24-27.

"Big Firm, Big Business, and Economic Progress," April 1965, pp. 39-42.

Similarly, to the editors and publishers of the following articles of mine go thanks for permission to include in this book material that appeared in:

"Invention in the Industrial Research Laboratory," *Journal of Political Economy*, April 1963, pp. 95-115, published by the University of Chicago Press.

"Size of Firm, Oligopoly, and Research: The Evidence," *Canadian Journal of Economics and Political Science*, February 1964, pp. 62-75.

D. HAMBERG

*Buffalo, New York*
*June, 1965*

# Contents

# Part 1

## The Research Explosion: Promise and Challenge

# 1 Growth and Distribution of Research and Development

Whether from hearsay or through the printed word in newspapers and magazines, virtually all readers are aware of the veritable explosion of expenditures on research and development (R & D) that has occurred in the United States economy in recent years. The magnitude of the current research effort and its rate of advance have inspired awe and generated a torrent of enraptured expletives describing the promise it holds forth in the form of lifesaving and life-serving new products and processes. How important technological change has been to our present living standards has recently been statistically verified in a number of independent studies. By various means, a succession of economists has estimated that between 50 and 90 percent of the advances in productivity (output per man-hour) in our economy have originated in technological progress.

To some extent these figures represent exaggerated claims for technical change, as all estimators are aware, for large improvements in the quality of the labor force and management and better organization have undoubtedly played a role of some importance in fostering advances in productivity and living standards. But only a casual comparison of the goods on the market and the production techniques used to make them today with the goods and techniques of yesteryear is enough to dramatize the contributions that inventions have made to our rapid advances in living standards.

With R & D being conducted on an unparalleled scale, the future is apparently filled with *potential* well-being on an equally unprecedented scale. I have underscored *potential* because it remains to be proved whether we shall indeed realize this promise. One of the interesting features of the recent research explosion, of the "technological revolution," is that it has thus far failed to show up much in the estimates of productivity growth. It is true that the growth rate of output per man-hour of 3.2 percent a year for the period 1947-64 was well above the long-term, 2.4 percent rate of increase. But it is also true that similarly high rates of productivity growth occurred in earlier periods for comparable lengths of time, and before the research explosion. And it is also true that the recent surge has been induced primarily by the great spurt in the growth of productivity in agriculture, where the reasons have had relatively little to do with the boom in research and development. In the 1947-64 period, productivity in the nonfarm, private sector grew at the average annual rate of 2.6 percent, versus a long-term rate of growth of 2.3 percent. In manufacturing, where R & D is concentrated, productivity advanced at the average rate of 2.8 percent a year, compared with a 2.7 long-term rate of increase.

Why productivity growth has lagged behind the great swell in R & D is hard to say, and efforts to evaluate the latter in these terms may be a bit premature. Nevertheless, it may be worthwhile to take a look at the overall character of the research explosion to see whether we can find clues, not only for the present and immediate past, but also for the foreseeable future. All that glitters may not be gold, and the realization of the promise may yet provide a challenge to private and public policy of which there is little awareness.

## The Magnitude and Character of the Research Explosion [1]

Because private industry has been conducting about 75 percent of all R & D, it may be well to begin our review of the record with an examination of what has been transpiring in this sector of the economy.

### INDUSTRIAL RESEARCH AND DEVELOPMENT

In 1961, private industry spent a total of $10.9 billion on R & D. Of this amount, $6.3 billion, or 58 percent, was financed by the Federal Government and the remainder by industry itself.

To get a glimpse of the rate at which industry R & D activity has grown, we may compare the 1961 total of $10.9 billion with the approximately $210 million spent in 1931, the $390 million spent in 1940, and the $2.2 billion total spent in 1951.[2]

---

[1] I have drawn principally on the following sources for the data reported below: National Science Foundation, *Research and Development in Industry 1961* (Washington, D. C., U. S. Government Printing Office, 1964) ; *idem., Reviews of Data on Research and Development* (Washington, D. C., U. S. Government Printing Office, 1963) ; N. E. Terleckyj, *Research and Development: Its Growth and Composition* (New York, National Industrial Conference Board, Inc., 1963) ; D. M. Keezer, "The Outlook for Expenditures on Research and Development during the Next Decade," *American Economic Review*, 46 (May 1960), 355-369. It should be observed that (as of June 1965) detailed data for 1961 are the most recently available.

[2] These figures are from Terleckyj, *op. cit.*, p. 104. On the basis of similar work, I judge Terleckyj's estimates to be by far the most accurate of the many estimates on the growth of R & D published to date.

Thus, between 1931 and 1961, industrial R & D programs increased fiftyfold (that is, 5,000 percent); and even between 1951 and 1961 the increase was 400 percent.

Much of this growth in industry's R & D spending, it must be noted, is exaggerated by inflation and changing definitions of research and development. Rapidly rising wages and salaries of researchers and cost of research plant and equipment have raised research costs tremendously, and broader definitions of research and development, induced partly by public relations factors and partly by tax law changes, both cause current dollar figures to overstate the increase in R & D activity in real terms. A variety of efforts to correct the current dollar figures, at least for cost increases, all reduce the increase between 1931 and 1961 by about one half. How much further the numbers would be reduced by correction for changing definition it is impossible to say. It is improbable that such further adjustments would reduce the increase much below twentyfold, and increases in industrial R & D activity of some 2,000 percent in 30 years are still extraordinarily impressive.

To get an idea of the breadth of industry participation in R & D, we may note that during 1961 the number of firms performing R & D was 11,800, of which about 10,300 were in manufacturing industries. In addition, many companies without R & D programs of their own supported projects performed by outside organizations.[3]

At the same time it should be noted that, these figures notwithstanding, industrial R & D is a highly concentrated activity. In 1961 the top 20 performing companies accounted for more than half of all R & D performed in the manufacturing sector

---

[3] In 1953, the last time figures were published in such detail, 20,000 firms in all industries participated in R & D, of which 3,700 without programs of their own supported projects performed by outside organizations.

of the economy, the top 40 companies accounted for 80 percent, and the top 300 for 91 percent.

Manufacturing industries, which accounted for only 30 percent of national income originating in all industries, conducted 98 percent of all R & D performed by industry. Table I shows, further, that two manufacturing industry groups alone, aircraft and missiles and electrical equipment and communication, performed 59 percent of all industrial R & D; but these accounted for a mere 6 percent of national income originating in all industry (20 percent of value added in manufacturing). The top six industries shown in Table I performed 87 percent of industrial R & D, but accounted for only 13 percent of national income.[4]

This last set of facts provides potentially important clues to the failure of the growth in productivity in the nonfarm sector of private enterprise to reflect the vastly increased tempo of R & D activities. One would expect this, with industrial R & D so heavily concentrated in the industries that account for such a small proportion of value added in the national economy. This situation tends to reduce greatly the potential zone of impact of R & D on the economy.[5]

[4] With the exception of aircraft and missiles, this distribution of industrial R & D is a continuation of a pattern that goes back at least to the twenties. See Terleckyj, *op. cit.*, p. 109. The recent ascendancy of the aircraft and missiles industry reflects, of course, the burgeoning defense and space programs.

[5] To the extent that the R & D results of one industry are embodied in products and processes purchased by other industries, as is notably true of purchases by agriculture, for example, this explanation may seem oversimplified. On the other hand, in 1958, the purchases of the manufacturing industries listed in Table I accounted for substantially more than half of interindustry sales of (relevant) intermediate products plus fixed capital goods, and since as a group they account for less than a third of value added by all industry, there is still probably considerable merit in the explanation. For a fine, overall evaluation of the impact of the R & D explosion on productivity, see E. F. Denison, *The Sources of Economic Growth in the United*

Moreover, the fact that some three fifths of all industry R & D is concentrated in the aircraft and missiles and electric equipment and communication industries is also very indicative. Most of the R & D performed by these industries is, of course,

**Table 1**  *Performance of R & D by Industry, 1961*

| Industry Group | R & D in Millions | Percent of Total Industry R & D |
|---|---|---|
| Aircraft and missiles | $3,957 | 37 |
| Electrical equipment and communication | 2,404 | 22 |
| Chemicals | 1,073 | 10 |
| Machinery, except electrical | 896 | 8 |
| Motor vehicles and other transportation equipment | 802 | 7 |
| Professional and scientific instruments | 384 | 4 |
| Petroleum refining | 294 | 3 |
| Primary metals | 160 | 2 |
| Rubber products | 126 | 1 |
| Fabricated metals | 118 | 1 |
| Food and kindred products | 105 | 1 |
| Stone, clay and glass products | 103 | 1 |
| Other manufacturing industries | 270 | 3 |
| Nonmanufacturing industries | 180 | 2 |
| Total, all industries | $10,872 | 100 |

SOURCE: National Science Foundation, *Research and Development in Industry 1961, op. cit.,* p. 9. Percentages may not total because of rounding.

associated with the nation's missile and space programs, and 85-90 percent of all R & D funds spent by these industries is on notoriously expensive development costs. To the dismay of many people (who, given the overwhelming importance of

*States and the Alternatives Before Us* (New York, Committee for Economic Development, 1962), pp. 239-249.

development costs in these areas, if for no other reason, perhaps should have known better), the spillover of results of R & D in these fields into the civilian economy has been small. Accordingly, in the face of the dominant importance of R & D in these industries, one would tend to be pessimistic about the potential impact of total R & D on the economy's productivity growth rate.

## FINANCE AND PERFORMANCE

It is also important to get some perspective on the place of industrial R & D in the total American research and development picture. We can best do this by examining some figures for the decade 1953-62. To begin with, we find that the major source of funds for financing all R & D activity has been the Federal Government, which supplied an average of 63 percent of all R & D funds during this period; most of this Federal spending, of course, was for defense and space purposes. Private industry, on the other hand, supplied an average of 35 percent of all R & D funds during this decade, and colleges and other nonprofit institutions 2 percent.

These figures stand in marked contrast with those of earlier years. In 1930, the Federal Government financed only 14 percent of total R & D activity, whereas private industry paid for some 70 percent, with nonprofit institutions accounting for the remainder. It is evident that important changes have occurred in the sources of R & D finance, mainly in the form of a shift from private to public sources. Inevitably accompanying this shift must have been a change in the pattern of incentives and controls governing corporate inventive activity. Whereas the bulk of it was distinctly profit-oriented and under the influence of the patent system and other social controls, evidently much of current industrial R & D is strongly influenced by political and defense considerations.

We can say this because no corresponding shift in the place where organized inventive activity is actually performed has occurred since 1930. During the period 1953-62, private industry performed an average of 75 percent of all R & D work, Government 15 percent, and nonprofit institutions 10 percent. Actually, these figures represent a 7 percent *rise* in industry's share of the conduct of all R & D work since 1930 (25 percent since 1920), mainly at the expense of the share of nonprofit institutions.

This pronounced difference in the sources of research funds and places of work is of course explained by the very large increase in Federal funds for research and development and the use of such funds to sponsor research in the private sector of the economy, primarily industry. In recent years, the Federal Government has been contracting 65 percent of its R & D funds to industry alone, with another 11 percent going to colleges and other nonprofit institutions.[6]

THE CONTENT OF RESEARCH AND DEVELOPMENT

It is also of interest to observe the character of the nation's R & D effort. The term *research and development* covers a multitude of activities, some of which are at best distant cousins to each other. Let us start by breaking down aggregate

[6] Reflecting, if not responsible for, the concentration of R & D performance in industry, Federal R & D funds to industry are extremely concentrated. Of the $6.3 billion paid to industry in 1961, 55 percent went to aircraft and missiles and 25 percent to the electrical equipment and communication industries. Also in Fiscal 1961, twenty corporations accounted for nearly 75 percent of total R & D contracts awarded by the Department of Defense; this department, in turn, accounted for approximately 75 percent of all Federal R & D contracts awarded in that year.

R & D activity into its major and familiar components. The first is research and the second is development. There is a world of differences in the nature of these two activities, important to bear in mind in interpreting R & D statistics, particularly because development expenditures tend on the average to run two to three times as high as research expenditures, often much more. Development begins where research ends, that is, where a model or invention has been proved technically feasible and has been designated for commercial (or military) application. Development then consists in bringing the successful invention to the point where it is ready for the market; it is the stage where prototypes are evolved, where technical problems of adjustment to "scale-up" are worked out and "bugs" are eliminated; in short, it is the pilot-plant stage where, largely through a process of trial and error, research findings are translated into products and processes ready for commercial or military application.

No derogation of the importance of the development stage is intended when we say that typically it involves a much lower order of inventive activity than research does; in fact, it involves little or no inventive activity. It often calls for great technical skill, engineering knowledge, and much resourcefulness. But it is not creative, or is so only to a minimal extent. Its task is essentially one of adaptation to or within known methods of production. The types and levels of talent required in development are thus distinctly inferior to those required to perform original and creative research and invention. Since development costs are so much greater than research costs, these facts are important to remember in evaluating expenditures that lump research and development together, especially in efforts to utilize aggregate R & D figures as measures of the level and growth of inventive activity.

We would be wise to limit our measures of inventive activity to the figures on research, which in its turn is usually broken down into two parts: *basic* and *applied* research. Basic research is ordinarily concerned only with the extension of the boundaries of knowledge, without any technological or commercial objectives in view. Applied research, in contrast, seeks new knowledge having specific technical and commercial applications in the form of new products and processes or improvements thereof. To a considerable extent, applied research builds upon the knowledge gleaned from basic and previously applied research; this is especially true in those areas of industry—for example, the chemical, petroleum refining, electric equipment, and electronics industries—where progress has rested upon advances in chemistry and physics. Surprising as it may seem, however, there are still many fields of industry that rest not on science, but on the older empirical arts—for example, the automobile, mining, and most household goods industries.

When it comes to collecting statistics on research and development, the lines between basic and applied research on the one hand, and the lines between applied research and development, on the other, are more difficult to ascertain than the above discussion would indicate. There is much division of opinion, even among experts, on the distinctions between these categories. Businessmen are frequently wont to characterize as basic research what experts would identify as applied research. More important, however, is the rather broad interpretation that business tends to give the term applied research. A company bringing out a lipstick of a new shade, or a new car, such as the unlamented Edsel or the compacts, will refer to these as new products and impute to them significant amounts of applied research. But clearly the amount of research that goes into such new products is small. Certain industries, such as the automobile industry, which ranks third (behind the chemical, electric equipment and communication industries) in unsubsidized spending on total research and development, with a figure in excess of $600 million, are notorious for their small expenditures on research relative to development. Beyond this, there is little doubt that companies generally include in their reported R & D figures the rather routine work associated with annual changes in model designs.

The foregoing remarks are intended as a warning of the many pitfalls that beset the prospective user and interpreter of published R & D estimates, particularly those involving breakdowns of R & D activities into their major components. They also suggest the nature of the lag that exists between our conceptual framework of these activities and the published data. Nevertheless, these data do give us rough ideas of orders of magnitude of the different categories of R & D and some insights into possible trends, information we shall find useful in later discussion.

In 1961, a total of some $15 billion, 2.9 percent of the gross national product, was spent in the United States economy on research and development (compared to about $300 million in 1931, which represented 0.4 percent of GNP in that year). Of this total about 70 percent was devoted to development alone, 22 percent went to applied research, and 8 percent went to basic research. These figures are reasonably representative of the distribution of total performance throughout the preceding decade, although there has been a discernible upward trend in the relative importance of development at the expense of both basic and applied research. Of course, the absolute amounts spent on all three activities have been rising sharply, but the rise in expenditures on development has outstripped the rise in research spending.

Of the basic research amounting to $1.5 billion in 1961, industry performed 27 percent and Government 16 percent, with colleges and other nonprofit institutions leading the list, not surprisingly, by performing 57 percent of all basic research. In the performance of $3.2 billions' worth of applied research carried on in 1961, industry led the way by conducting 63 percent of the work; but surprisingly, and possibly dangerously, colleges and other nonprofit institutions, the traditional bailiwick of basic research, conducted as much as 20 percent of applied research work, with Government accounting for the remaining 17 percent. In the conduct of development in 1961, industry did most of the work, 84 percent, Government performed 12 percent, and colleges and other institutions 4 percent. All these figures are fairly representative of the distribution of the performance of R & D during the preceding decade.

It will also be instructive to examine the distribution of the different categories of R & D activities *within* these sectors of the economy, particularly within the industrial sector, because it has been performing approximately three quarters of all research and development activity, and also within the nonprofit, institutional sector because of certain disturbing trends there. Of the almost $11 billion worth of research and development work performed by industry in 1961, 78 percent was on development, 18 percent on applied research, and only 4 percent was on basic research. (Industry financed out of its own pocket 78 percent of all the basic research it performed and 24 percent of all basic research done in the economy.) Although these figures, too, approximate the corresponding averages for the previous decade, the relative importance of applied research fell by about 10 percent between 1951 and 1961.

Turning now to the colleges and other nonprofit institutions, we find that in 1959-60, 43 percent of the $1.2 billion total research and development performed in this sector was on basic research, 39 percent on applied research, and 18 percent on development. The relative importance of applied research and development is surprising enough in a sector that has been a major source of advances in basic science. What is even more a cause for concern is the 9 percent drop in the relative importance of basic research in this sector since 1950 and the 14 percent drop since 1945. The entirety of this drop is explained by the 30 percent rise in the relative importance of development activity in this sector since 1950 and the 70 percent rise since 1945.

Thus the outstanding feature of these aggregate and sector figures on research and development is the drop in the relative importance of basic research and applied research, both giving way to development. By way of emphasizing the extent of this shift in the composition of research and development, especially at the expense of basic research, it is worthwhile drawing a comparison with some earlier figures. During the 1920's, colleges and other nonprofit institutions accounted for approximately 20 percent of all R & D expenditures and during the 1930's for about 15 percent. Before World War II these groups, especially the colleges, confined their activities almost exclusively to basic research; industry and Government also performed some basic research, but in quite marginal amounts. Hence we can use the figures for nonprofit institutions as estimates of the relative importance of basic research in the total R & D picture during the interwar decades. In 1961, by comparison, spending on basic research accounted for only 8 percent of total R & D, a decline of some 60 percent from the 1920's and almost 50 percent from the 1930's in the relative importance of this strategic activity. Only the Government sector has not shared in this decline. Since 1945, at least, basic research has hovered between 8 and 11 percent of total research and development performed in this sector.

### The Place of the Independent Inventor

Before we leave this review of the R & D record and pass on to
a discussion of some of its implications, it is worth noting a
major gap in the available statistics, so far as they are interpreted as a measure of current inventive activity. They exclude
the work of the independent inventor, whether full-time or part-
time. And there is good evidence that the inventor working
outside the industrial laboratory is still a prime source of major
inventions.

In support of this statement, we may cite the well-known
study of inventions headed by Professor Jewkes.[7] This study
sought the origins of sixty-one important inventions made since
1900. Of the sixty-one about two thirds were made after 1930,
and over 40 percent were made after 1940. Thirty-three of the
sixty-one inventions (or 54 percent) were the product of the
work of independent inventors and included such inventions as
air conditioning, automatic transmissions, Bakelite (the first
commercial plastic), cellophane, the helicopter, the jet engine,
catalytic cracking of petroleum, the continuous casting of steel,
quick freezing, and streptomycin.

We have also conducted a study of major inventions of recent vintage only, specifically inventions made during the decade 1946-55. The origins of twenty-seven such inventions were
investigated, and of this number twelve (or 44 percent) originated in the work of independent inventors. These included
the ENIAC, the oxygen converter, stereophonic sound, neomy-
cin, natural-color television, Systox, prestressed concrete, and
hot extrusion of steel.

[7] J. Jewkes, D. Sawers, and R. Stillerman, *The Source of Invention* (London, Macmillan and Co., 1958), particularly pp. 72-88 and Part II.

A study of patent data by Professor Schmookler indicates that as many as 50-60 percent of today's inventors are outside the organized research groups of the corporate industrial laboratories.[8] Other data reveal that in the seven-year period 1950-57, an average of 16,000 patents was issued to independent inventors. Although there is probably considerable variation in the quality of these patents, it is interesting to note that the patents of independents are used commercially about as frequently as those originating in the industrial research laboratories of the large corporations.

Nevertheless, if the patent statistics are a good indicator, the independent inventor has fallen greatly in importance as a source of inventions, absolutely and relatively. The 16,000 average number of patents issued to independents in the early fifties represent but one half the peak reached in 1916. Moreover, in 1900 over 80 percent of all patents were issued to independents and less than 20 percent to corporations. In 1957, independents obtained but 36 percent of the total, corporations 61 percent, and Government 2 percent.

Many people have wondered whether the decline, often exaggerated, in the relative importance of the independent inventor and the rise in the importance of the hired inventor have made obsolete the term inventor. Their point is usually twofold: (1) With so much invention currently being undertaken by groups of specialists, pooling their knowledge and skills from divers fields, and joining in a cooperative venture, the designation of a specific individual as the inventor often be-

[8] J. Schmookler, "Inventors Past and Present," *Review of Economics and Statistics*, 39 (August 1957), 321-33. This study showed that 40 percent of the patentees were not technologists and hence presumably not in the employ of research laboratories. In addition, only some 40 percent of the patentees were full-time hired inventors, the remainder having been line technologists, executives, and individuals in divers occupations. Also, 50 percent of the patentees were not college graduates and therefore presumably not members of the skilled teams in the industrial research laboratories.

comes increasingly difficult, if not impossible. (2) The same problem arises from the increasing dependence of any particular discovery on a host of prior advances in knowledge, without which the one in question would be impossible. In short, any invention occurs through the accretion of details rather than as major creations *de novo*.

Dealing with the second point first, we may observe that it has been characteristic of virtually all inventions from time immemorial. Even when the solo inventor completely dominated the scene, his inventions surely built upon prior knowledge and experience. In this sense, nothing has changed in the field of invention. At the same time, a person (or group) who can conceive of a new combination of old ideas—and usually in the process incorporate new ideas, with the result that something radically new is born—has clearly made an original invention. Certainly, Bell, Marconi, and Edison, to list a few well-known names, were strongly beholden to prior advances in knowledge stemming from previous basic and applied research performed by others; but these earlier advances did not produce a telephone, radio, or incandescent lamp. It took the creative genius of these men to combine the earlier elements with novel ones of their own in a unique way to produce these inventions.

In some cases, it is true, a succession of individuals and groups has been responsible for strategic developments that were later embodied in the final product, with only marginal advances contributed by the individual or group credited with the invention. The invention of the diesel electric engine (commonly credited to General Motors), fluorescent lighting (commonly credited to General Electric), and rockets (accurately credited to a number of names) are cases in point. Others of a similar character could be mentioned, but so could a large number be added to the earlier list of names easily identified with well-known inventions (such as Gillette, of safety razor fame, Carrier, inventor of air conditioning, and Armstrong, inventor of FM radio). In short, it seems best to avoid being dogmatic on the point of identification of inventors and to treat each invention as a separate case. In any event, the problem is not new.

But the importance of groups cooperating in joint research ventures, if not absolutely new, has certainly grown to unprecedented proportions. What of *the* inventor in these circumstances? Obviously, the answer is that such a designation does tend toward obfuscation and obsolescence. However, let us note that group invention tends to be concentrated in those areas amenable to scientific research. As observed earlier, there are still many areas of technology not yet firmly grounded in science, areas where the empirical arts still dominate. Such fields embrace most consumer goods, many industrial techniques, and much mechanical equipment. Independents have contributed many important advances in the automobile, in steel ingot production techniques, and so forth.[9]

Moreover, it is well to caution against the reputed virtues and results of group research. There is much evidence to indicate that many of the apparent products of group research turn out to be chiefly the results of one principal researcher surrounded by a group of laboratory assistants and working with a minimum of elaborate equipment. Freon refrigerants, tetraethyl lead, and nylon are examples of products discovered in these circumstances, and in each case one person is easily identifiable as the real inventor.

[9] Patent data indicate that independents are responsible for 88 percent of mechanical inventions and only 9 percent of electrical and 3 percent of chemical inventions. These data, it may be noted, exclude patents issued to independents who have incorporated themselves, as many do; hence the figures on electrical and chemical inventions, the former particularly, understate the proportion of the inventions attributable to independents.

Nevertheless, the question of identifying the inventor is often troublesome under conditions of organized research, and will probably become more so with the passage of time. Already it has given rise to questions of the relevance of the patent system, with its emphasis upon the protection and reward of the independent inventor, in an era in which so many inventors work in groups and under conditions widely at variance with those that prevailed during the first 175 years or so of the patent system.

With these remarks, we conclude our survey of the research and development situation as it exists in the United States. What are some of the more important implications of these developments for private and public policy alike? It is to this question that we turn our attention in Chapter 2.

# 2 *Implications of the Research Explosion*

That there has been a research explosion there can be little doubt. The discussion in the last chapter revealed that in current dollars both industrial and total R & D increased some fiftyfold between 1931 and 1961. This discussion also disclosed (1) a heavy preponderance of development work as opposed to research and a distinct downward trend in the relative importance of research, especially basic research; (2) a radical shift in the sources of R & D funds from private to public sources; and (3) a rise in the relative importance of industrial R & D activity, *vis-à-vis* both other areas of organized R & D and the independent inventor as well.

## The Neglect of Research

No doubt readers will have read and heard before of the relative neglect of research, particularly basic research, in the United States economy. But to learn that basic research in 1961 comprised but 8 percent of total R & D, 4 percent of industrial R & D, and but 43 percent of that performed by colleges and other nonprofit institutions must come as something of a shock. During most of our history we have been known as laggards in the performance of basic research, and have been renowned for our reliance on Western Europe's advances in basic science. Yet we have found a startling and alarming decline of 50 to 60 percent in the relative importance of basic research in our overall R & D effort since the 1920's and 1930's.

The extreme imbalance between basic research, on the one hand, and applied research and development, on the other, poses a real danger to the future productivity of applied research and development. When industry can draw on well-advanced basic science, the costs in time and effort of applied research and development can be expected to be much lower than otherwise. Basic scientific breakthroughs often facilitate the discovery of inventions previously deemed impossible or extremely difficult; they are no less important in speeding up and cheapening development, the costs of which we have found to loom so large in our total R & D effort. The alternative to operations from an advanced scientific base is to employ expensive and time-consuming practical and empirical methods.

It is no accident either that the nation's R & D effort is concentrated in so few fields, such as the aerospace, electric equipment, and chemical industries. These industries all operate on more or less well-developed scientific bases. Almost without exception most of our remaining industries, which conduct next to no R & D or, like the auto industry, notoriously low-level R & D, operate on the basis of little basic science.

It is important, then, that when we rejoice in the magnitude and growth of our R & D effort we be sure what we are rejoicing about. The quality of our research effort is, or should be, a cause for worry, for basic research is obviously still being undersupported and underemphasized. There are many reasons why this is so. In industry most firms simply refuse to support much basic research. One reason is that it takes too long to pay off, and most firms prefer investments with a short pay-out period. More important, perhaps, is the fact that the fruits of basic research are highly uncertain, uncertain as to outcome in general and as to the ability of the sponsoring firm to exploit a specific discovery. Although proposals have been made for stimulating industry participation in basic research through special tax incentives and forms of subsidy, such incentive schemes offer little promise. The reason is almost inherent in the nature of basic research: lacking a specific commercial or technical objective, it is next to impossible to determine what will come out of it, and very few companies are so diversified that they can use whatever is discovered. There are surely advantages to firms engaging in basic research, in the form of rises in the intellectual tone of industrial laboratories and therefore higher-caliber applied research and development, the attraction of better scientists and engineers, and a link with the scientific community and funnel for new ideas and scientific information. Despite these advantages, the performance of basic research in industry is likely to be limited to a few large and highly diversified companies—most of them defense contractors.

It appears that we shall have to continue to look to the universities and Government for the required increases in the future conduct of basic research. This being the case, the 14 percent decline since 1945 in the relative importance of basic research, accompanied by the 70 percent rise in that of development, among the colleges and other nonprofit institutions must arouse dismay, especially since there has been no offsetting increase in the conduct of basic research by Government.

Ironically, the Federal Government itself bears a heavy responsibility for the shift away from basic research by the universities. Since World War II, the Government has been exerting pressure on the universities to conduct programs relating mainly to engineering and development problems associated with defense needs. As a result, these institutions have been drawn into the hardware end of research and development on an unprecedented scale. Of course, the deterioration of the financial situation of the universities, consequent upon the effects of inflation on incomes from endowed funds and on operating costs, combined with soaring enrollments, have caused them to welcome the availability of these Government R & D funds, even to seek them out. Many university professors, anxious to supplement their incomes, have been equally receptive to such Government grants, even to the extent, in some cases, of compromising their main research interests or changing their research fields to secure them. Hence the free, roving speculation in search of new, truly basic knowledge, which it is the duty of universities to carry on, has been displaced in part by an atmosphere encumbered by the pressures of problem-solving for Government agencies.

The trend toward Government-supported-and-directed research in the universities has also had its counterpart in a large increase in applied research and development sponsored by industry. Indeed, many university science and engineering departments are deeply immersed in various forms of industrial research and engineering consulting. Thus it is clear that both industry and government are in the process of squeezing the lifeline on which the long-run viability of their future R & D programs must ultimately depend.

These activities have had other insidious effects that bode ill for the future quality of our nation's R & D effort. Graduate students, the source of our future supply of scientists and technologists, are directed to work along conventional lines instead of encouraged to undertake new departures in basic research. As a result, we are faced with the danger of being confronted with a class of educated hacks, deprived of the top-notch scientists who are responsible for great intellectual break-throughs and who would fortify and advance all our future R & D efforts.

It is clear that if the research revolution is to be maintained and its quality raised, it must be enriched by more basic research activity than we now support. In the end this will likely entail a vastly increased subsidy program for basic research, mainly to the universities to enable them to resist the attractions of Government and industry research contracts and to retain and expand their scientific staffs and basic research programs. And Government and industry both had better quickly revise their present practices of deflecting interest from truly basic scholarship. The universities cannot fail in the conduct of this crucial function, for no other agency in our society can be counted on to take up the slack.

It may be wise to close this part of the discussion by also issuing a warning about the need for industry to raise the level of its *applied* research programs. We have already indicated how loosely this term is bandied about in industry and of what a low order much applied research is. There is strong evidence that industry tends to concentrate too much on applied research that features the short payoff.[1] As a result, much of its inventive activity is concerned with marginal improvements, featuring process and product development. Considering how much money industry has been spending on R & D, it is truly astonishing how few major, radically new inventions have originated in this sector, especially among the large firms. It is evident that far too many resources are being devoted to development activities and routine design improve-

[1] See below, pp. 77-79.

ments that have been dignified by the term research. Reasons for the low quality of industry's applied research effort are discussed at length in Chapter 5 below. But if industry insists on diverting scientific and technical personnel from other activities, it is time it became more aware of the social responsibilities to which it claims to be alive. For in the long pull, it is the basic inventions from applied research that, combined with the fruits of basic research, maintain the stream of technical progress.

### The Need for Changes in the Patent System

As a result of the rapid rise in the relative importance of industrial R & D performance and the radical shift from private to public sources of R & D funds, an increasing swell of discontent with our patent system has been occurring. The traditional argument for the patent system, namely, that the prospect of monopoly profits it provides is necessary to induce inventors to undertake the risks and expense of invention and innovation—the commercial exploitation of inventions—is said to have become obsolete. In the current business milieu, industry conducts R & D and innovates not under the stimulus of the patent system, but under the stimulus of competition. Competition, in the form of new and improved, and lower-priced, products and processes, among firms has become the principal spur to the growth in organized R & D. Technological advances have become a major instrument in the struggle for market positions among the industrial firms of our economy. Outlays on R & D are now made because producers cannot afford to lag behind their innovating competitors if they want to stay in business and also because the reputation of a firm rests heavily on its ability to keep ahead, to be first in the market with something new and first in price reductions (if any)—or at least last in price increases. Moreover, for important new inventions producers can rely on the temporary monopoly-profit incentives from the natural head start that their own innovations give them over their competitors and from the time lag that is necessary before competitors can catch up.

No less important a source of disenchantment with existing patent arrangements has been the rise in Government R & D finance to a point where 55 to 65 percent of the funds for industrial R & D performance has been coming from the Federal Government. Perhaps the most notable feature of Government-sponsored R & D is the total absence of all financial risk on the part of the firms conducting the R & D. No matter how difficult or expensive a project turns out to be, the costs are covered by the Government on a cost-plus basis of one sort or another; the contracting firm pays not one cent from its own pockets. Furthermore, there is no market to be developed. The market is there, waiting eagerly, in the form of the Federal agency for whom the R & D has been performed. And if, as has been true in many cases, there are commercial applications of the inventions issuing from Government-financed R & D, the performing firm gets first crack and, with the accumulated know-how, a head start over potential competitors.

Yet, despite the total absence of risk and the inevitable accrual of built-in competitive advantages, most Government R & D contracts permit the performing company to secure patent rights to inventions developed under Federal sponsorship. Here is a clear-cut case in which society gets none of the alleged advantages of the patent system, because with no risks patent rights are clearly not needed to serve as an inducement to invent and innovate; at the same time, society suffers all the disadvantages of the patent system.

And there are many disadvantages. The numerous abuses of the patent system aside, there are drawbacks that *inhere* in this system, and it is these drawbacks that have been inviting much of the recent criticism. The first of these is the limitation placed on the rate of diffusion of new inventions by the restricted use of inventions that patents permit their owners. The range of application of new inventions is thus necessarily narrower than it would be otherwise. As a result, most firms are cut off from the most advanced technology and are thereby forced to produce poorer-quality products with poorer-quality techniques. Even the quality of their research is necessarily poorer, because it must be based upon knowledge that existed prior to that incorporated into existing relevant patents. Any effort to incorporate and build upon knowledge contained in extant patents (other than that patented by the prospective inventor) entails patent infringement. Hence, not only is the diffusion of existing knowledge and techniques limited, but the ability to extend the boundaries of knowledge is also obstructed and retarded.

Combined with the pressures of competition, this first disadvantage of the patent system leads to a second inherent one. A primary motive behind today's industrial—unsubsidized—research effort is the desire to enlarge, or at least preserve, the performing company's share of the market. When one firm discovers a new or improved product or process, its competitors are bound to follow suit. But when the first has obtained a patent, the competitors are forced to *invent around* this patent in order to compete with the patentee in the same market. Inevitably, then, much industrial research involves a wastage of resources, in time, effort, and facilities, as firms seek alternative ways of doing what is already technically and commercially feasible. Only occasionally does this duplication result in something better. In most cases, society would benefit much more by devoting the same resources to enlargement of the boundaries of scientific and technological knowledge.

What are the alternatives to the present operation of the patent system? Specifically, how can it be brought up to date to accord with the large rise in the relative importance of industrial research and the big shift in sources of finance from private to Federal funds? At one extreme, we have the suggestion that the patent system be abolished altogether in order to maximize the range of applications of all inventions. This proposal suggests, in effect, that all knowledge be made a free good. Although such a proposal possesses considerable merit, its achievement through the simple abolition of the patent system would be subject to two serious objections. One is that some part of applied research (remember that the results of basic research are nonpatentable) is very expensive and highly uncertain as to outcome. This type is probably in need of the extra spur provided by the possibility of temporary monopoly profits that accrue from patents. The other reason is that the patent is the only form of protection to the solo inventor, who is still of considerable importance as a source of major inventions. The patent is the only thing of substance the solo inventor can sell, his only basis for claim to a reward for his invention.

To meet these objections, but at the same time to make knowledge a free item so as to maximize its use, it has also been suggested that the patent system be abolished *and replaced* by a system of awards from the public trough. By making new scientific and technological knowledge free thereafter, a system of Government awards would place such knowledge on the same status as old and all other nonpatentable knowledge, so that there would be no economic deterrent to the former's use. All incentives for *inventing around* new inventions would also be eliminated, and the waste of very scarce resources in duplicate research would stop. The difficulty with this suggestion, of course, lies in the problem of establishing a system of awards that would be free of arbitrariness. Yet the system of awards under the patent system is filled with arbitrariness, too, and it is a shame that the proposal for public awards has not received the serious attention that it merits.

Still another suggestion for improvement and updating would modify the present patent system by the issuance of dual patents. Long-term patents, like the 17-year ones presently issued, would be limited to those involving major technological breakthroughs because they are of great value, and ordinarily the research involved is of the type that is very costly and uncertain in outcome. The more common types of improvement inventions, the kind that typically evolve out of the research fostered by competitive pressures, would be granted patents of much shorter duration. (They might even be denied patent protection altogether on the grounds that no extra inducement, over and above the forces of competition, is needed to stimulate the conduct of this type of research. The Supreme Court has, indeed, suggested such an approach.) Creating a class of petty patents for minor inventions would not only tend to reduce many of the difficulties discussed earlier, but would also eliminate much harassing infringement litigation; it would also strike at industrial monopolies built upon indiscriminate acquisition of large aggregates of patents or by the continual acquisition of new patents *in seriatum* as a means of perpetuating supposedly temporary monopoly positions built up under expired patent privileges.

Administrative difficulties would arise under this system, too, but nonetheless it rates serious consideration, particularly since comparable administrative difficulties have plagued the present patent system since its inception. (The "degree-ofnovelty" test under the present system is a major case in point.)

Probably the least radical, but not necessarily the best, suggestion for accommodating the patent system to the modern era would simply eliminate the granting of patents on inventions arising out of Government-sponsored research; the Government would simply retain title to all patent rights in these cases. In the interests of maximizing the use of the new knowledge developed in connection with such research, as well as avoiding the worst defects of the patent system, the Government would then issue nonexclusive, royalty-free licenses to all comers. In this case, it is argued, no violations of the principles of the patent system would occur, because with the contractors relieved of all financial risks, these principles are inapplicable in the circumstances. Moreover, substantial advantages accrue to contractors from Government-financed R & D that are quite independent of patent privileges and in many instances are apparently more important to companies than patent rights.[2]

Nevertheless, there is one potentially critical, implicit assumption underlying this proposal that bears examination. The assumption is that there are neither further development costs nor little risk involved in commercial innovation of the Government-sponsored inventions. In many instances this assumption would hold up and has quite evidently done so. But where inventions need much additional and expensive development and their future profitability is clouded with uncertainty, firms may be unwilling to bear these costs and risks without exclusive licenses to Government-owned patents, which may lie unused.

Evidently, this possibility calls for a flexible approach in

2 Some of these extra advantages are described below, pp. 124-125.

the handling of Government-owned patents. The proper approach is suggested by the experience of the Research Corporation, a company that markets patents for universities, apparently with great success. This company sells its patents mainly on a nonexclusive basis. However, when there are no acceptances of nonexclusive patents and when development costs appear to be very large, in a small number of cases exclusive rights have been granted for a limited period, not in excess of five years. Here, then, is a model that might be used in establishing an appropriately flexible system of managing Government-owned patents.

There seems to be little doubt that it is time for a change. A nation that has shown as much ingenuity in adapting to technical change as ours should be able to do as much in adapting to social and economic change. The conditions surrounding our patent system are very different from those that marked its inception. Any one of the foregoing proposals provides a sound basis for cautious experimenting designed to bring this system into the middle of the twentieth century.

# Part 2 | Market Structure and Economic Progress

# 3 *Size of Firm, Industry Concentration, Research, and Innovation*[1]

For many years, the defense of the giant corporations possessing considerable monopoly power in an oligopolistic setting[2] has been rooted in the argument that both were the product of a technology that requires large-scale enterprises for efficient production. In brief, the economies of mass production are supposed to give rise to optimal-scale firms that are too large, relative to the size of markets, to permit the large num-

[1] This chapter is a revision of my paper, "Size of Firm, Monopoly, and Economic Growth," *Hearings of the Joint Economic Committee of Congress on Employment, Growth, and Price Levels: Part 7, The Effects of Monopolistic and Quasi-Monopolistic Practices* (Washington, D. C., U. S. Government Printing Office, 1959), p. 2337.

[2] For readers who may be unfamiliar with the term oligopoly we may note that it means, literally, few sellers. *Fewness* is a situation in which each of the sellers controls enough of total industry output so that variations in the output and price by any one of the sellers affect both his sales and also those of his rivals. This ability to influence market price is what is meant by monopoly power. But the fact that *rivals'* sales will also be affected, and thereby invite uncertain retaliatory action by them, is the distinguishing feature of oligopolistic price behavior. In an effort to avoid the uncertainties surrounding the effects of independent price changes by each of the sellers, there is a strong tendency to avoid price competition altogether, and to divert such competitive proclivities as remain into channels like advertising and other forms of sales promotion and product variation.

ber of sellers needed to minimize monopoly powers over prices and production.

Although still possessing many adherents, this defense of the giant corporation has recently fallen from favor, primarily for lack of empirical support. In its place has come a new one. The large, monopolistic firms, we are now told, have become the principal sources of economic progress; on the one hand, they are now conducting most of the research on and development of new and improved products and processes that are the backbone of economic growth;[3] on the other hand, even when important inventions have not originated in their own laboratories the large companies have been mainly responsible for carrying out the major innovations of recent decades.

Because of the importance of this subject in the arena of public policy, a brief examination of the a priori arguments for and against this new defense of the corporate giants and concentrated production is in order, to be followed, in the next two chapters, by a look at the evidence to see what light it has to shed in what heretofore has been a dark corner.

### In Defense of Bigness

To begin with, the new defense of the giant monopolistic company argues that the cheap and simple inventions have already been made. Modern advances in science and technology require skilled teams of scientists and engineers, working in splendidly equipped laboratories and supported by various

---

[3] This widely held belief is a great exaggeration. The giant corporation is undoubtedly the principal conductor of *organized* research, i.e., research that takes place in organized laboratories established for this purpose. But it is evident that a good deal of inventive activity occurs outside these organized laboratories. This point is discussed on pp. 16-17.

types of ancillary personnel. And only the giant corporation has the resources to finance these prerequisites to the discovery of new knowledge and techniques. To the extent that major innovations entail expensive pilot plants, new and equally expensive plant and equipment, costly sales campaigns, and so forth, again it is only the giant corporation that has the resources to bear these costs. Moreover, such companies can afford to employ executives with the drive and imagination to originate, develop, and exploit new ideas and ways of doing things.

Financial strength gives the giant corporation other decisive advantages in the conduct of R & D, the defense continues. Thus the high risks of failure in the various stages of research and development—and innovation, too—are well known. The great financial and technical resources of the giant firm, however, enable it to support many R & D projects simultaneously, with the result that it is in an excellent position to pool the risks of failure. When only a few projects are undertaken, there is always the possibility that the results will be total failure. But the conduct of a large number of projects carries with it reasonable assurance that some will succeed and yield a return that will compensate for the failures. A large number of projects also reduces the chance that successful ones will be anticipated by rivals.

The ability of the financially strong giant firms to weather economic hardship is also well documented. In turn, this means that such firms have almost unlimited life expectancies. Consequently, because they expect a long life, they can wait longer for the payoff; in other words, they can and do have comparatively low discounts for time and uncertainty.

A large firm is also typically a diversified one; that is, such firms are usually multiproduct firms. This characteristic offers still another big advantage toward the successful conduct of

R & D programs. In many cases even if a research project is successful, uncertainty exists whether the outcome will fall within the firm's range, such as production know-how, sales contacts, and other requirements. But the larger and more diversified a firm is, the more likely it will be to have the ability to use the results of its research. And to the extent that such firms also have access to large markets, can afford to pay for advertising in important media, have highly developed distribution outlets and high-priced sales personnel, their ability to use the results of the research successfully is greatly enhanced.

Finally, there are the incentives offered by the concentration of production and sales implied by the terms monopoly and oligopoly. Ultimately the profits from R & D on new and improved products come from sales, of course. And the larger the share of the market a firm has, the larger the proportion of total sales and profits it can hope to capture. In the case of cost-reducing, new—or improved—processes, concentration in production also holds forth the promise of sufficient volume to make the unit-cost savings sufficient to pay for the preceding investments.

These same incentives are perhaps even more needed as an inducement to firms to invest in the production and sale of new and untried products and techniques of production. And clearly, unless there are incentives to introduce commercially new products and processes—that is, to innovate—there is no incentive to spend on the R & D from which these result. At the same time, innovational investment is often more risky and expensive than invention. Therefore, excess profits associated with substantial monopoly power are needed to foster innovation. Without the protective shield of such monopoly power— or contrariwise with the prospect of quick and easy imitation and vigorous competition—the incentive to undertake risky and expensive innovations would evaporate.

On the basis of such arguments, a number of economists have concluded that an industry composed of a few large firms will conduct more R & D and innovate more readily than a more competitive industry characterized by numerous comparatively small firms.[4]

## *Against Bigness*[5]

As usual, there are at least two sides to every question, and this is no less true of the role of the giant corporation and monopoly power in the invention and innovation processes. For one thing, the large corporation can lead, and has led, to developments not conducive to the risk-taking that is associated with innovation. Chief among these is the emergence of bureaucratic organizations of officials to carry out the multiple complex functions inherent in modern, large-scale enterprise. The bureaucrats of the large corporations, usually cloaked with substantial monopoly power, develop a strong sense of security about their positions, a career attitude toward managerial positions that makes it imperative to be good team men and

[4] Some of the leading references to these various facets of the new defense of the giant corporation and monopoly power are: J. A. Schumpeter, *Capitalism, Socialism, and Democracy* (New York, Harper and Brothers, 1942); J. K. Galbraith, *American Capitalism: The Concept of Countervailing Power* (Boston, Houghton Mifflin, 1952); A. D. H. Kaplan, *Big Enterprise in a Competitive System* (Washington, Brookings Institution, 1954); and most recently, H. H. Villard, "Competition, Oligopoly, and Research," *Journal of Political Economy*, 66 (Dec. 1958), 483-97.

[5] Many of the arguments against the new defense of the giant corporation per se as a conductor of R & D are, in effect, criticisms of *organized* research as carried on in the research laboratories of these corporations. As such, these arguments are discussed at length in Chapter 5 below. Hence, for the most part we shall limit the discussion here to the arguments against monopoly power in the innovation process.

follow the accepted rules of action and behavior.[6] These are not the qualities of the prospective innovator. Risky ventures are avoided that might destabilize existing market situations and threaten the position of the entrenched managerial bureaucracies, which operate better in a stable environment than in a changing one. These bureaucracies tend to become instruments of resistance to rather than promoters of change.

Moreover, it must be remembered that inventions and innovations that are substitutes for existing products and processes involve losses from the scrapping of existing plant and equipment. Firms protected by monopoly power may be expected to avoid such losses by postponing innovation until existing capital goods have depreciated considerably. Why render obsolete with a new innovation what the company has struggled to build up? And this is no less true of firms that spend large sums on research than of those that do not. In fact, the former may aim much of their research at the protection of existing monopolistic strength as well as at the avoidance of capital loss through obsolescence, by obtaining patents ahead of others threatening the firm's entrenched position. Scrutiny of the innovational behavior of the electric lamp, radio and television, railway locomotive, and telephone industries, among others, discloses that innovations of competitive products have occurred only after long periods of market exploitation of old products. The investigations of a number of writers have brought them to the conclusion that new firms are very often needed if radically new innovations are to take place; this has been true even in industries where the established firms have

---

[6] For interesting and incisive discussions of the extent to which these qualities of corporation executives are being emphasized, see V. Packard, *The Hidden Persuaders* (Philadelphia, David McKay Co., 1957), Chapter 18; and W. H. Whyte, *The Organization Man* (Garden City, N. Y., Doubleday & Co., 1956), Parts I-IV.

had reputations for progressiveness, such as the electric lamp and telephone industries.[7]

This information should not be unexpected. Innovation is certainly expensive and risky. The intelligent and informed management figure is all too aware of this, particularly if he has recently experienced the trials and tribulations of innovation and market consolidation. Following this experience, a period of quiescence is apt to be the most attractive situation. With good profits and monopoly powers that may insulate well against potential competition, executives are prone to refrain from innovation, to be content with protecting the fruits of past efforts. They are hardly likely to destroy one innovation soon afterwards with a new one.

Monopoly power also impairs the ability of new firms, firms that by their very nature are likely to be aggressive innovators, to enter an industry with new and cheaper techniques or new, substitute products. Sometimes the monopolistic firm obstructs such entry by deliberate action, as by threatening destructive price competition, patent-shelving, expensive and drawn-out patent litigation, controls over supplies of raw materials, and so forth. At other times, the mere strength of the firm's hold on the market may act as a strong deterrent to the entry of new firms.

Whatever the means, monopoly power automatically reduces the number of centers of organized research by limiting the number of firms in an industry. As a result, the probability of investigating any given research opportunity is reduced.

[7] See W. R. MacLaurin, *Invention and Innovation in the Radio Industry* (New York, The Macmillan Co., 1949) ; A. A. Bright, *The Electric Lamp Industry: Technological Change and Economic Development, 1800-1947* (New York, The Macmillan Co., 1949) ; R. Schlaifer and S. D. Heron, *The Development of Aircraft Engines and Fuels* (Cambridge, Mass., Harvard Business School, 1950) ; and R. R. Nelson, "The Economics of Invention: A Survey of the Literature," *Journal of Business,* 32 (April 1959), 108-109.

Similarly, in consequence of the reduction in the number of possible buyers, the market for independent inventions is reduced.

For these and other reasons it is possible that potential capacities of the giant monopolistic firm to conduct research and carry through innovation are neutralized by other factors that act as a restraint on economic progress. So let us turn now to the argument that monopoly power is a necessary incentive to research and innovation because the prospect of excess profits stemming from such power is needed to induce potential innovators to undertake the great risk and expense that are often associated with research and innovation. If potential imitation is quick and easy, it is averred, there is little inducement to accept the possibility of losses.

There is probably a good deal of merit in this reasoning, and of course upon it rests the basis for the patent system, which is certainly one of the outstanding but widely accepted forms of monopoly power. However, even granting the validity of this form of monopoly power, this is quite different from granting the general validity of all forms of monopoly power, even for economic progress. In examining the role of monopoly power in economic progress, it is necessary to make a proper distinction between those *temporary* forms that may be needed to induce investment and the more general and *established* forms of such power that threaten to, and often do, stifle progress. For there is nothing in established monopoly power as such that necessarily constitutes a source of incentive to innovate; on the contrary, there is much to smother progress. If established monopolies or oligopolies remain progressive, this may probably be traced to the persistence of competitive pressures, or possibly chance attributes that make management interested in invention and innovations.

Even in the case of the supposedly temporary monopolies

granted by patents, there are many instances of strong innovative activity without them, or with patents of dubious value, because the original inventions were subject to such close imitation as to negate their exclusive value. This knowledge should make us wonder whether the value of even the patent system and its temporary monopoly power has not been exaggerated.[8] Whatever the merits of such temporary forms of monopoly power, however, one thing seems certain. There are enough cases of inventions and innovations by firms possessing little or no monopoly power as to cast in serious doubt most of the suggestions that established monopolies are a necessary or even an important ingredient of economic progress.

The one feature of large business size and monopoly power that appears to carry potential weight is associated with the usually large—absolute—profits of the big monopolistic firms as a source of funds to finance research and innovation. However, it would be improper to infer from this that company size must be of a magnitude comparable to that of United States Steel, General Motors, Standard Oil of New Jersey, or National Dairy Products to be able to finance R & D. In 1961, the average cost of an R & D scientist or engineer was $35,000.[9] Thus a company with annual sales of some $9,000,000 spending the industry average of some 4 percent of sales could afford a group of ten such personnel plus their technical assistants, and others. A company of this size is a far cry from the giants who pose the threat of excessive monopoly power.

Further, the alleged financial advantages of the large monopolistic firm in the conduct of research and innovation are simply one aspect of the well-known differential access to

[8] See above, pp. 26-27.
[9] National Science Foundation, *Research and Development in Industry 1961* (Washington, D. C., U. S. Government Printing Office, 1964), Table A-28.

finance of small and large firms. To recognize this finance problem, however, is not necessarily to condone giant size and monopoly power as the solution. Financial aid to small business of the sort envisioned in the establishment of the Small Business Administration and the recent expansion of its activities offers a more hopeful and worthy solution. But such programs must be carried out on a much larger scale if they are to succeed in promoting competition and economic progress alike in the national economy.[10]

[10] The interested reader will find further discussions of the counterarguments to the new defense in the following: J. Jewkes, D. Sawers, and R. Stillerman, *The Sources of Invention* (London, Macmillan and Co., 1958); P. Hennipmann, "Monopoly: Impediment or Stimulus to Economic Progress?" in E. H. Chamberlain, ed., *Monopoly and Competition and Their Regulation* (London, Macmillan and Co., 1954), p. 421; G. W. Nutter, "Monopoly, Bigness, and Progress," *Journal of Political Economy*, 64 (December 1956), 520-527; and J. Schmookler, "Bigness, Fewness, and Research," *Journal of Political Economy*, 67 (December 1959), 628-635.

# *4* Size of Firm, Industry Concentration, and Economic Progress: The Evidence

Having examined arguments for and against the new defense of the giant corporation possessing considerable monopoly power, we can examine the various kinds of evidence that is now available on what is obviously a controversial subject. In this way, we can see where the weight of the evidence appears to lie. The reader may then be able to form his own conclusions on a matter that patently has broad ramifications for social policy in general and antitrust policy in particular.

We shall first examine the evidence bearing on R & D, evidence that is now fairly abundant. Less is available bearing on innovation. However, there is enough to warrant at least some consideration at this time.

## *The Evidence: Research and Development*

The evidence to be presented on R & D is of the following types: (1) statistical evidence on relations between industrial R & D activity, in both absolute and relative forms, and size of firm; and (2) statistical evidence on the relation between

R & D, absolute and relative, and the degree of industry concentration.

## ABSOLUTE R & D AND SIZE OF FIRM

Data published by the National Science Foundation lend solid support to the thesis that R & D activity increases with size of firm. Among manufacturing companies as a group, some 90 percent of the firms employing more than 5,000 people conduct R & D; from this level the figure falls steadily until it reaches about 8 percent for companies employing less than 100 people. What is true for manufacturing industry as a whole also appears to hold for individual (two- and three-digit SIC [Standard Industrial Classification]) industries.

Other data show R & D expenditures to be heavily concentrated in large companies. In 1961, for example, companies employing fewer than 1,000 people spent about 5 percent of total R & D funds in industry and those employing between 1,000 and 5,000 people spent 9 percent, whereas firms employing 5,000 or more people accounted for 86 percent of industry spending on R & D; and this last group has apparently been steadily increasing its share over the years. This size-distribution, too, holds among individual industries.[1]

The last set of figures, it is true, relates to R & D performance, not to its financing; as a result, the figures are biased somewhat by the tendency of the Federal Government to

[1] See National Science Foundation, *Science and Engineering in American Industry* (Washington, D. C., U. S. Government Printing Office, 1956), Tables A-2 and A-3; *idem., Funds for Research and Development in Industry 1958* (Washington, D. C., U. S. Government Printing Office, 1961), Table A-10; *idem., Science and Engineering in American Industry* (Washington, D. C., U. S. Government Printing Office, 1959), Table A-2; *idem., Research and Development in Industry 1961* (Washington, D. C., U. S. Government Printing Office, 1964), Table A-1.

concentrate its R & D contracts heavily in large companies. Nevertheless, the percentage distribution of strictly company-financed R & D is also highly skewed in favor of large firms. In 1961, companies with fewer than 1,000 employees accounted for 7 percent of this source of R & D finance, those in the 1,000-4,999 class accounted for 13 percent, with companies employing 5,000 or more people accounting for 80 percent of the total.[2] It is also worth noting that the most active R & D performers are much less important as a group in their share of total employment; in 1958 their share of total R & D cost was some 84 percent, and their share of total employment was 29 percent (41 percent of manufacturing employment).

It seems fairly evident that size of firm is a very important determinant of R & D activity—when firms of *all* size classes are considered. However, there is evidence of considerable variation in the conduct of such activity among the larger firms in a number of industries. Hence it seems worthwhile to investigate the influence of size more closely, specifically by examining the relation between R & D activity and size among the larger firms only. Such information is obviously important in any effort to understand how far the element of size in the new defense may be pushed. If, for example, the influence of size on the conduct of R & D is much smaller among the larger firms than among firms of all size classes, then there may be room for many more firms in an industry than would be the case if the influence of size is very great among the larger firms as well—when the conduct of R & D alone is considered.

To this end, we have gathered together data on this subject for 340 large firms in seventeen two- and three-digit industry

[2] National Science Foundation, *Research and Development in Industry 1961*, *op. cit.*, Table A-8.

groups in the manufacturing sector for the year 1960. Because data on R & D expenditures by individual firms are not published, we have used the data on numbers of R & D personnel published by the National Research Council.[3] The list of 340 firms is based on that of *Fortune* magazine's 500 largest industrial firms in 1960 (published as a supplement to the July 1961 number) for which R & D personnel data were available. Other industry groups (two-digit) were excluded because of insufficient numbers to allow reliable statistical results. In addition, of the 340 firms studied, only four employed 2,000 people or less in all operations.[4]

Well-known problems arise in the choice of an appropriate size variable. The National Science Foundation uses total employment as its size variable in reporting R & D expenditure data. To provide a measure of consistency with both the earlier data and the R & D data used here, we too have used total employment as a size variable. But equally well-known differences in capital intensity (capital-labor ratios) have given rise to objections to the accuracy of total employment as a measure of size of firm. To reduce the possibility of bias in results on this account, as well as to give the reader his choice, we have also conducted our statistical analyses using total assets as the size variable. The results based on both size variables will be presented.

Another problem arises in the choice of the correlation techniques here employed. When the number of items observed is small, least-squares correlation coefficients are not very reliable, and in a number of our industry groups we were faced with this problem. Furthermore, wide differences in the value

[3] *Industrial Research Laboratories of the United States,* 11th ed. (Baltimore, Waverly Press, 1960).

[4] One firm in primary metals employed 1,000 people, two in petroleum and petroleum products employed 800 and 900 people respectively, and one in food and kindred products employed 2,000.

of size variables can give rise to spurious correlation results. Therefore, we have made estimates of rank-order correlations. But since these have limitations of their own, we have also computed least-squares correlations and shall present coefficients based on both methods.

Finally, we may note that each firm was classified in a single industry on the basis of its major product activity.[5] Since many companies with large R & D programs have establishments located in a number of different industries, the industry data presented below are not directly comparable with industry data aggregated on the basis of an establishment reporting unit.

With these preliminaries out of the way, we present below in Tables 2 and 3 the industry rank-order and least-squares correlation coefficients respectively for R & D personnel, and the two size variables just discussed. Before these statistics for the individual industries are examined, however, the least-squares correlation coefficients for the variables under analysis for 387 large companies lumped together in one group may be of interest; these companies cover sixteen two-digit industries in manufacturing, plus three two-digit public utility industries, as well as the communication industry.

Correlating R & D personnel with total employment for the 387 companies *en masse* yielded a least-squares correlation coefficient of .69, which was significant at the .01 level in a one-tailed test. Thus, in this case size explains 48 percent of the variance in R & D employment. With assets as the size variable the correlation coefficient obtained was .55, also significant at the .01 level; in other words, 30 percent of the vari-

---

5 Based on product-line information contained in *Poor's Register of Directors and Executives, 1960* (New York, Standard and Poor's Corp., 1960), which gives four-digit product classes for each company, and *Moody's Industrial Manual, 1960* (New York, D. F. Shea, 1960).

ance in R & D employment is explained by size when assets
are the size variable.

For industry as a whole, there is clearly some positive relation between R & D employment and size among the largest
firms; therefore, we may infer that a tendency does exist
among the largest firms in the economy for R & D activity to
increase with size.[6] Nevertheless, the association can hardly
be described as very strong and is noticeably weak with assets
as the measure of size. At least for large firms as a whole, too
much of the variance in R & D employment is left unexplained
by the size variables to permit us to attribute more than a
modicum of weight to size as a determinant of R & D.[7]

In part, this conclusion, as well as others that follow, rests
on a judgment about where to draw the line between strong
and weak correlations. The present writer is inclined to draw

---

[6] Positive correlation, of course, does not mean causality. Nevertheless, I
think it is fair to presume that the direction of causality in this case has
run from size to R & D activity, because in most cases it seems clear that
the firms were large before they got into R & D at all or in a big way. And
I would apply this stricture to the results obtained in the analysis of the
same relations in the individual industry groups.

[7] The statistics reported above may be compared with those reported by Ira
Horowitz in "Firm Size and Research Activity," *Southern Economic Journal*
28 (January 1962), 298-301. Horowitz employed data on 700 companies
surveyed by the National Association of Manufacturers in 1947 and on 4,800
surveyed by the Harvard Business School in 1951 and 1952. For 18 two-digit
industries in the NAM survey and 29 two- and three-digit industries in the
Harvard survey, Horowitz ranked industries on the basis of average employment size per establishment and value added per establishment. Then, also
ranking the industries on the basis of percent of respondents maintaining
research organizations, he obtained rank-order correlations between this
measure of research inclination and each of the size variables, using the
Kendall rank-order correlation method. The Harvard data yielded correlation coefficients of .31 for both size variables, with both results significant
at the .05 level. The NAM data yielded coefficients of .51 with employment
as the size variable and .55 with value added as the size variable, and both
these statistics were significant at the .05 level. Evidently, research inclination is also positively associated with size of firm, but the association is not
particularly strong.

**Table 2** *Rank-order Size Correlation Coefficients for R & D in Nineteen Manufacturing Industries, 1960* [a]

| Industry Group | No. of Firms | Employment | Assets |
|---|---|---|---|
| Aircraft and parts | 21 | .72 | .61 |
| Chemicals and allied products | 56 | .81 | .73 |
|    Industrial chemicals | 27 | .90 | .74 |
|    Drugs and medicines | 12 | .53 | .80 |
|    Other chemicals | 17 | .58 | .59 |
| Electrical equipment | 30 | .76 | .75 |
| Fabricated metals | 17 | .55 | .90 |
| Food and kindred products | 56 | .59 | .70 |
| Machinery (except electrical) | 45 | .69 | .60 |
|    Extractive, construction, and conveyance equipment | 15 | .73 | .69 |
|    Machine tools and special industry machinery | 10 | .82 | .76 |
|    Other machinery | 20 | .58 | .49 |
| Paper and allied products | 19 | .74 | .74 |
| Petroleum and petroleum products | 26 | .92 | .89 |
| Primary metals | 33 | .57 | .56 |
| Stone, clay, and glass products | 19 | .89 | .59 |
| Motor vehicles and other transportation equipment (except aircraft) | 18 | .83 | .73 |
| Textiles and apparel | 13 | − .06 | .26 |
| Professional and scientific instruments | 7 | .61 | .43 |

[a] For this table only, correlation coefficients were computed for the textiles and apparel and professional and scientific instruments industries, even though they fell short of the numerical requirements for two-digit industries established at the outset. The chemical and machinery industries were broken down into three-digit classifications because of their high ranking in industrial R & D (dollar) performance figures and the large number of firms we had for these two (two-digit) industries—in order to extract additional information. However, the data for the three-digit machinery industries should be taken with a grain of salt, because of the unlikely product categories that have been paired.

this line at a correlation-coefficient value of .80; but I think it would be difficult to defend a value of less than .70 as the point of demarcation. In any case, the reader is free to draw his own conclusions from the statistics presented.

**Table 3**  *Least-squares Size Correlation Coefficients for R & D in Seventeen Manufacturing Industries, 1960* [a]

| Industry Group | No. of Firms | Employment | Assets |
|---|---|---|---|
| Aircraft and parts | 21 | .72 | .68 |
| Chemicals and allied products | 56 | .87 | .86 |
|     Industrial chemicals | 27 | .88 | .86 |
|     Drugs and medicines | 12 | .59 | .80 |
|     Other chemicals | 17 | .87 | .80 |
| Electrical equipment | 30 | .64 | .55 |
| Fabricated metals | 17 | .93 | .93 |
| Food and kindred products | 56 | .47 | .49 |
| Machinery (except electrical) | 45 | .58 | .52 |
|     Extractive, construction, and conveyance equipment | 15 | .77 | .72 |
|     Machine tools and special industry machinery | 10 | .80 | .79 |
|     Other machinery | 20 | .64 | .61 |
| Paper and allied products | 19 | .50 | .49 |
| Petroleum and petroleum products | 26 | .84 | .80 |
| Primary metals | 33 | .76 | .79 |
| Stone, clay, and glass products | 19 | .87 | .77 |
| Motor vehicles and other transportation equipment (except aircraft) | 18 | .96 | .96 |

[a] The remarks about the three-digit industry groups in the machinery industry in Table 2 apply to this table, too, as well as those that follow.

Now let us turn to an analysis of the correlation coefficients for the separate industry groups shown in Tables 2 and 3. Because I am inclined to place more trust in the rank-correlation coefficients, for reasons mentioned earlier, I shall concentrate mainly on these, but once again the reader can follow his own judgment. With total employment as the size variable, and with all correlations except that of the professional and scientific instruments industry significant at the .05 level in a one-tailed test, some positive correlation between this variable and R & D personnel is clearly present in all but one of the nineteen two- and three-digit industries presented in Table 2, the lone exception being textiles and apparel. Among the two-digit industries, the correlation is especially strong in the petroleum and stone, clay, and glass products industries, where about 80 percent or more of the variance in rank order of R & D personnel is explained by rank order of total employment; not far behind are the chemical and transportation equipment (except aircraft) industries, where size accounts for some two thirds of variance in R & D personnel. Among the three-digit industries, size is very important in industrial chemicals, which apparently accounts for the importance of this influence in the chemical industry as a whole, and somewhat less so in the industry group producing machine tools and special industry machinery. Among the remaining industries, employment size is less important, ranging in its explanation of rank-order R & D personnel variance from .28 (drugs) to .58 (electrical equipment). If the reader will accept as *weak* correlations of less than .70, and as *fairly strong* correlations of .70-.79, then in nine industry groups (six two-digit and three three-digit) the association between employment size and R & D may be characterized as weak, and in four groups (three two-digit and one three-digit) as fairly strong.

With total assets as the measure, the influence of size on the employment of R & D personnel declines somewhat, although positive association between these two variables is clear in all industry groups except textiles and apparel and professional and scientific instruments, where, in addition to being very small, the rank correlation coefficients are not significantly greater than zero at the .05 level in a one-tailed test. (All the others are.) The number of two- and three-digit industry groups in which the correlation between size and R & D personnel can be described as strong (correlation coefficients of .80-1.0) declines from six to three. The entirety of this decline shows up in an increase from four to seven in the number of industry groups in the range we have characterized as displaying fairly strong association. Of the ten industries where the choice of size variable makes a significant difference, the shift to assets causes the influence of size to decline in seven instances and rise in three.

The petroleum industry continues to exhibit strong association between size and R & D, even with assets as the size variable, making the influence of size on the conduct of research in this industry virtually unassailable. Most notable among the industries in which the size influence increases with the shift to assets are the fabricated metals industry, where the proportion of explained variance in rank-order R & D employment rises from 30 to 81 percent, and the drug industry, where this same proportion rises from 28 to 64 percent. Among the industries in which the influence of size decreases with the shift to assets, the most notable is the stone, clay, and glass products group, where the proportion of rank-order variance in R & D explained by size drops sharply from 79 to 35 percent. By our criterion of strength of association, the influence of size is visibly affected downwards in the aircraft and industrial chemicals industries. Regardless of the size variable employed, and by almost any standards, the influence of size on R & D employment is weak in the machinery (especially with respect to assets), primary metals, textiles and apparel, professional and scientific instruments, and other chemical groups.[8]

Although the reader may wish to check this for himself, I think it is fair to say that, with few exceptions, no striking differences arise in the results stemming from the use of least-squares (as opposed to rank) correlation techniques. Comparing the figures in Tables 2 and 3, we find that the use of least-squares correlation methods produces a notable increase in the influence of size in three industry groups (fabricated metals, motor vehicles and other transportation equipment except aircraft, and other chemicals) and a decrease in two industries (electrical equipment and paper and allied products). Irrespective of these differences, however, positive association between the size variables and R & D employment is patently in evidence in both tables.

The conclusion is inescapable, then, that among the large companies R & D employment tends to increase with size of firm. At the same time, there is considerable variation among industry groups in the strength of this association for both size variables, but the association appears to be somewhat stronger when total employment is the measure of size. Lumping together the results of both size variables, we can say, on the basis of the probably more reliable rank correlations, that in eight out of nineteen two- and three-digit industry groups the association between size and R & D employment can be described as strong, in the sense that size can explain about two thirds or more of the variance in R & D.

A reader may object to this last statement on the grounds

---

[8] There is evidence of an increase in the influence of total assets on R & D employment between 1950 and 1960. Compare the results of Table 2 with those reported by J. S. Worley, "The Changing Direction of Research and Development Employment Among Firms," in Universities-National Bureau Conference, *The Rate and Direction of Inventive Activity: Economic and Social Factors* (Princeton, Princeton University Press, 1962), p. 245.

that the two-thirds criterion of strength of association is wholly arbitrary. This is necessarily a matter of judgment. Therefore, instead of engaging in endless debate on a matter for which there are no hard and fast rules, I propose to probe deeper into the influence of size by examining its association with R & D *intensity,* that is, the *relative* amount of R & D undertaken among the larger companies. The reason is that unless R & D intensity is highly correlated with size among the large firms of an industry, concentrated production in the form of, say, oligopoly may not be the prescription for fostering industrial research.

RESEARCH INTENSITY AND SIZE OF FIRM

The basis for the last statement may be put as follows: If in a given industry the proportion of the total number of firms spending a given percentage of, for example, sales on R & D is constant, regardless of the number of firms, then the ratio of *industry* R & D to sales will also be constant, irrespective of the number of firms in the industry. In this case, a reduction in the number of firms will not improve industry performance, provided the smaller number of now larger firms each devotes the same proportion of sales to R & D as did the previously larger number of smaller firms, even though the proportion of all firms conducting R & D is unchanged.

Turning the matter around, we can say that it may be possible to increase the number of firms in an industry (perhaps by dissolution of the largest) without sacrificing any R & D in that industry. In the latter case, this will be true even in the unlikely event that some of the smaller new ones cease R & D altogether; so long as the remainder together with the other performers of R & D comprise the same proportion of all firms in the industry and continue to spend on R & D at the same rate, total industry spending on R & D will be of the same proportions.[9]

Admittedly, the conditions of this case limit its generality. If large firms in various industries spend a significantly larger percentage of their sales than do small ones, as is generally true,[10] then a reduction in the number of firms, with a concomitant increase in production among the larger ones, *may* stimulate R & D.[11] But if among the *larger* firms only there were no statistically significant difference in R & D intensity, this would suggest severe limits to the degree of industrial concentration as a means of stimulating R & D; in other words, the conditions of our case would be closely approximated. In short, the case for oligopoly (bigness and fewness) would certainly be much stronger if R & D intensity were a positive function of size among only the larger firms in an industry.[12]

To obtain evidence on the relation between R & D intensity and size among the larger firms, we have made use of the earlier data to estimate correlations between the ratio R & D employment/total employment and total employment and assets for (1) the same 387 larger companies as a group described

[9] A numerical example may make this point clearer: If 60 percent of 20 firms (or 12) spends 1 percent of sales on R & D and 60 percent of 30 firms (or 18) also spends 1 percent of sales on R & D, total industry spending on R & D in both cases will equal 0.6 percent of sales.

[10] See National Science Foundation, *Research and Development in Industry 1961, op cit.,* Tables A-22 and A-24.

[11] But see below, pp. 63-64, where statistical analysis indicates a weak relation between R & D and oligopoly.

[12] My argument also assumes that the percentage of firms performing R & D is invariant with respect to the number of firms in an industry, and this is also rather clearly untrue. However, data I have assembled on some 700 firms indicate that in the vast majority of manufacturing industries, at least for the year 1960, once companies approach total employment of 5,000 people, the percentage of such firms in an industry conducting R & D reaches a constant 100 percent. Other data, of the National Science Foundation for 1958, bear this out. See National Science Foundation, *Funds for Research and Development in Industry 1958, op. cit.,* Table A-10.

earlier and (2) the same 340 large companies distributed among the same industry groups as earlier.

First, we report the least-squares correlation coefficients for the 387 companies *en masse*. Correlating the ratio R & D employment/total employment with total employment yielded a least-squares correlation coefficient of .45, which was significantly greater than zero at the .01 level in a one-tailed test. Correlating the same R & D intensity ratio with total assets yielded a correlation coefficient of —.01, which was not significant at the .05 level. When employment is the size variable, therefore, there is evidently some positive association between R & D intensity  and size among the larger firms for industry as a whole, but it is rather weak, only 20 percent of the variance in R & D intensity being explained by size. With assets as the size measure, there is no evidence of positive association whatever.[13]

To test for the influence of size on R & D intensity among the 340 large firms in each of seventeen two- and three-digit industry groups, rank correlations were run between the same pairs of variables as those used for the 387 companies across the board. The results are shown in Table 4. Among the total employment coefficients, only those for the industrial chemicals, machine tools and special industry machinery, petroleum, stone, clay, and glass products, and the motor vehicle and other transportation equipment industries are significant at the .05 level in a one-tailed test, and among the asset coefficients only those for the fabricated metals, food and kindred products, machinery, machine tools and special industry machinery, and petroleum industries are similarly significant.

[13] To see whether any better results would obtain with the use of an R & D/ *sales* ratio, the least-squares correlations were also run for the ratio of R & D employment/sales against total employment and assets. The respective correlation coefficients were .037 and —.024, and neither was significant at the .05 level.

**Table 4** *Rank-order Size Correlations for R & D/ Employment in Seventeen Manufacturing Industries, 1960*

| Industry Group | No. of Firms | Employment | Assets |
|---|---|---|---|
| Aircraft and parts | 21 | .33 | .20 |
| Chemicals and allied products | 56 | .17 | .19 |
| Industrial chemicals | 27 | .39 | .24 |
| Drugs and medicines | 12 | −.35 | −.08 |
| Other chemicals | 17 | −.01 | .14 |
| Electrical equipment | 30 | .30 | .31 |
| Fabricated metals | 17 | .34 | .55 |
| Food and kindred products | 56 | −.13 | .28 |
| Machinery (except electrical) | 45 | .31 | .29 |
| Extractive, construction, and conveyance equipment | 15 | .34 | .34 |
| Machine tools and special industry machinery | 10 | .70 | .67 |
| Other machinery | 20 | −.04 | −.09 |
| Paper and allied products | 19 | −.22 | −.13 |
| Petroleum and petroleum products | 26 | .64 | .62 |
| Primary metals | 33 | −.20 | −.20 |
| Stone, clay, and glass products | 19 | .47 | .29 |
| Motor vehicles and other transportation equipment (except aircraft) | 18 | .51 | .38 |

With the possible exception of the petroleum and machine tools and special industry machinery groups, the relation between R & D intensity and size of firm is evidently very weak. The proportion of variance in rank-order R & D intensity is explained by size ranges from 0 to 49 percent, regardless of the size variable used.[14]

[14] Using R & D employment/sales as the measure of research intensity yields little difference in the results. Ranking industries in the same way described in footnote 7, and using R & D *expenditures*/sales as the measure of research intensity, Horowitz ("Firm Size and Research Activity") ob-

Following a suggestion by Worley,[15] we may undertake a more general analysis of the influence of size of firm on research intensity by estimating regression equations for each industry of the form

$$Y = AX^b,$$

where Y is R & D employment, and X is, separately, the size variables total employment and total assets. For computational convenience, this equation may be converted to its logarithmic equivalent

$$\log Y = \log A + b \log X.$$

For present purposes, the values of $b$ command our attention. Remembering that regressions will be fitted to data for large firms only, the reader will note that the values of $b$ should significantly exceed 1 if, beyond certain limits, increased concentration of industry is to stimulate the conduct of R & D. (For a value of $b$ greater than 1 means, of course, that R & D intensity is an increasing function of size of firm.) To determine whether the computed values of $b$ measure up to this requirement, we may subject them to a $(t)$ significance test on the basis of the null hypothesis that the true value of $b$ equals 1 in each industry and thereby determine at what level the estimated values of $b$ are significant.

The estimated values of $b$ for each of the size variables, total employment and assets, are shown below in Table 5, with the levels at which they are significant, in a one-tailed test, given in brackets immediately below each regression coefficient. With

---

tained a rank correlation coefficient of .31 (not significant at the .05 level) with average employment as the industry size variable and .40 with value added per establishment as the size variable (significant at the .05 level), on the basis of the NAM data.

[15] J. S. Worley, "Industrial Research and the New Competition," *Journal of Political Economy*, 69 (April 1961), 183-186.

total employment as the size variable, and on the basis of a .05 level of significance, the value of $b$ is significantly greater than 1 in the petroleum and stone, clay, and glass products industries (where it is so even at the .01 level of significance).[16] Interestingly, the value of $b$ is significantly *less* than 1 in the primary metals industry, meaning that in this industry group the relation between research intensity and size as measured by total employment is inverse. Although of uncertain reliability, the results reported in footnote 16 indicate the same relation holds in the textile and professional and scientific instrument industries.

With total assets as the size variable, only in the fabricated metals and petroleum industries is the value of $b$ significantly greater than 1 at the .05 level of significance; in petroleum this is true even at the .01 level, apparently making the influence of size on R & D intensity in this industry virtually unchallengeable. Once more, however, in the primary metals industry the value of $b$ is significantly less than 1.

In summary then, a case can be made for the hypothesis that research intensity (as measured by the ratio R & D employment/total employment) increases with size among the larger firms in but three industries. In the remaining 14 (or possibly 16) industries that we have scrutinized, there is no solid evidence in support of the hypothesis. In one industry group, primary metals, on the basis of the rank correlation tests as well as the regression analyses, the conclusion seems warranted that increased concentration may well *reduce* industry conduct of R & D, since the evidence is strong of an inverse relation be-

---

[16] Inadvertently, regressions were run also for the textiles and apparel and the professional and scientific instruments industries; so for what they are worth, we report the estimated values of $b$ with their levels of significance in parentheses. With employment as the size variable, $b = .017$ (.05) and .515 (.05) in the textiles and instruments industries, respectively. In the same order, with assets as the size variable, $b = .480$ (.20) and .664 (.10).

**Table 5** *Estimated Values of Regression Coefficient,*
b, *and Levels of Significance for Seventeen*
*Manufacturing Industries, 1960*

| Industry Group | No. of Firms | Employment | Assets |
|---|---|---|---|
| Aircraft and parts | 21 | 1.300 | 1.170 |
| | | (.20) | (.30) |
| Chemicals and allied products | 56 | 1.156 | 0.987 |
| | | (.10) | (.50) |
| Industrial chemicals | 27 | 1.157 | 0.981 |
| | | (.10) | (.50) |
| Drugs and medicines | 12 | 0.609 | 0.983 |
| | | (.10) | (.50) |
| Other chemicals | 17 | 1.082 | 0.819 |
| | | (.40) | (.30) |
| Electrical equipment | 30 | 1.291 | 1.142 |
| | | (.10) | (.30) |
| Fabricated metals | 17 | 1.185 | 1.466 |
| | | (.40) | (.05) |
| Food and kindred products | 56 | 0.767 | 0.993 |
| | | (.20) | (.50) |
| Machinery (except electrical) | 45 | 1.249 | 1.218 |
| | | (.20) | (.20) |
| Extractive, construction, and conveyance equipment | 15 | 1.390 (.20) | 1.281 (.30) |
| Machine tools and special industry machinery | 10 | 2.212 (.10) | 1.600 (.20) |
| Other machinery | 20 | 0.891 | 1.039 |
| | | (.40) | (.50) |
| Paper and allied products | 19 | 0.712 | 0.763 |
| | | (.10) | (.20) |
| Petroleum and petroleum products | 26 | 1.397 | 1.156 |
| | | (.01) | (.01) |
| Primary metals | 33 | 0.665 | 0.600 |
| | | (.05) | (.02) |
| Stone, clay, and glass products | 19 | 1.842 | 1.125 |
| | | (.01) | (.50) |

| Industry Group | No. of Firms | Employment | Assets |
|---|---|---|---|
| Motor vehicles and other transportation equipment (except aircraft) | 18 | 1.304 (.10) | 1.229 (.20) |

tween R & D intensity and size among the larger firms. In any case, it seems clear that increased concentration of industry beyond certain limits cannot be counted upon, in most cases, to act as a spur to the conduct of R & D.

RESEARCH AND INDUSTRIAL CONCENTRATION

To test further and more specifically the influence of industrial concentration per se on the conduct of R & D, least-squares and rank correlation tests were performed on the relation between (1) industry aggregates of company-financed (absolute) R & D *expenditures* and indicators of industrial concentration, and (2) company-financed industry R & D/sales ratios and the same indicators of industrial concentration, all the data being for the year 1958.[17]

The least-squares and rank correlations between absolute

[17] I am indebted to one of my former students, John Murphy, of Canisius College, for carrying out these correlations—in connection with a paper presented to my seminar in the Economics of Technological Change. The data on absolute R & D expenditures are from National Science Foundation, *Funds for Research and Development in Industry, 1959* (Washington, D. C., U. S. Government Printing Office, 1962) Table A-8; the data on R & D/sales ratios are from *idem., Funds for Research and Development in Industry, 1958, op. cit.*, Table A-26. The data on industry concentration are from *Concentration Ratios in Manufacturing Industry*, Report by the Bureau of Census for the Subcommittee on Antitrust and Monopoly of the Committee on the Judiciary, United States Senate (Washington, D. C., U. S. Government Printing Office, 1962).

R & D spending and industrial concentration were .56 and .46 respectively, both coefficients being significant at the .05 level in a one-tailed test. As earlier, I am inclined to treat the rank correlation as more accurate, in this case because of the great differences in the values of the "average concentration indicator" (the largest of which was almost 4.5 times bigger than the smallest). However, it doesn't seem to make much difference which one chooses, because while both indicate some positive association between industrial concentration and R & D, both reveal a rather weak association. Although the rank coefficient indicates that merely 21 percent of the variance in industry R & D spending is explained by industrial concentration, the least-squares coefficient raises this proportion of explained variance to only 32 percent.[18]

Correlating the R & D/sales *ratios* with industrial concentra-

---

Briefly, Murphy obtained his "weighted average concentration indicator" for each industry by weighting the percent of shipments in each (five-digit, SIC) product class accounted for by the four largest companies and summing the results for each (two- and three-digit) industry group; each sum was then divided by the corresponding sum of weights to obtain the weighted average concentration indicator for each industry group. These were correlated with the R & D data for twenty two- and three-digit manufacturing industry groups. Further details on Murphy's procedure will be available in a forthcoming paper.

[18] Ranking industries on the basis of the concentration ratio for sales of the four largest firms in an industry, and correlating these ranks with others based on the percent of respondents maintaining research organizations, Horowitz ("Firm Size and Research Activity") obtained rank correlations of .40 with the Harvard data and .60 with the NAM data, both significant at the .05 level. On the basis of well-known critiques of the common approach to the measure of industrial concentration used by Horowitz, critiques which Murphy (see note 17) tried to meet with his measure, I am inclined to place more credence in the latter's results, although both reveal too much variance in industry R & D spending left unexplained by industrial concentration to attach much importance to the latter variable as a determinant of R & D.

tion did not yield substantially different results. The least-squares coefficient was .54 compared to a rank coefficient of .36, with the first, but not the second, coefficient being significant at the .05 level.[19] At most, therefore, 30 percent of the variance in R & D intensity is explained by industrial concentration, while the proportion of explained rank-order variance is much less. Hence though positive association between R & D intensity and industrial concentration apparently exists, it must be described as weak—and with it the case for industrial concentration as a stimulus to R & D—both in absolute and relative terms.

### The Evidence: Innovations

For evidence on the relation between size of firm, market structure, and innovations, we must draw on the recently published work of Professor Edwin Mansfield, who has been conducting a number of detailed statistical studies in this area. Because the relevant data are often hard to generate in the quantity that all of us would like, Mansfield's results must often be interpreted as strongly suggestive rather than definitive. But they represent the results of careful work, and more important, they are virtually the only evidence we have on the subject at issue.

Studying twelve important innovations in four industries (bituminous coal, iron and steel, brewing, and railroad), Mansfield found some evidence that when the rate of return and the size of the investment in an innovation are taken into account (in a multiple correlation and regression analysis), the rate of

---

[19] With the same measure of industrial concentration as that described in footnote 18, and with R & D/sales as his intensity measure, Horowitz ("Firm Size and Research Activity") obtained a rank correlation of .38 (significant at .05) with the NAM data.

diffusion of an innovation within an industry was higher in more competitive industries.[20]

On the basis of the same twelve innovations plus two more, in the same four industries, Mansfield also found that when the profitability of an innovation was taken into account, larger firms tended to introduce new techniques faster than small firms.[21] However, he obtained this result only when he pooled all his data for purposes of statistical estimation. When he treated each innovation separately, Mansfield found that the relation between size of firm and speed of response to new techniques was often nonsignificant, statistically speaking.[22] This difference in results is important to bear in mind. Pooling data from different groups, in this case industries and innovations, often hides significant differences among the groups in the degree of association between variables.[23]

Aside from the influence of size on speed of response of firms to new techniques, Mansfield has also come to grips directly with the hotly disputed question whether the corporate giants have been the leading innovators of new techniques.[24] Specifically, he examined the relation between the percentage of important innovations made by the four largest firms of an in-

[20] E. Mansfield, "Technical Change and the Rate of Imitation," *Econometrica*, 29 (October 1961), 752-753 and *passim*.

[21] E. Mansfield, "The Speed of Response of Firms to New Techniques," *Quarterly Journal of Economics*, 77 (May 1963), 297-298 and 302.

[22] For the uninitiated, this means that there was a probability greater than 1 in 20 (i.e., .05) that the positive effect of size of firm on the speed of response was due to chance. Few, if any, statisticians will accept as statistically significant a result that may be due to chance with a probability greater than .05. The same meaning may be imputed, incidentally, to the .05 significance levels repeatedly referred to in the earlier discussion of the relation of size of firm to R & D, etc.

[23] For a similar difference involving the degree of association between the size of firm and research, see pp. 49-54, 58-59.

[24] E. Mansfield, "Size of Firm, Market Structure, and Innovation," *Journal of Political Economy*, 71 (December 1963), 560 ff.

dustry and their share of the market for the prewar and post-war periods; this was done for three industries: iron and steel, petroleum, and bituminous coal. On the basis of admittedly crude measures, Mansfield's data show that in the petroleum and coal industries the share of innovations in both periods exceeded the market share of the four largest firms,[25] while the reverse was true in the steel industry.

Crude though these results are (note that in the two cases where there is overlap with my researches on R & D) the results are consistent. Thus my earlier data showed that petroleum was the one industry where R & D intensity indisputably increased with size of firm, even among the large firms; *ceteris paribus,* we would expect the large firms in these circumstances to produce more than their share of innovations. Similarly, our earlier data showed the basic metals industry to be the one case where R & D intensity fell as size of firm increased. This result accords with Mansfield's showing the share of innovations of the four largest firms to fall short of their market share.

Also on the basis of admittedly "extremely crude" methods, Mansfield sought to determine whether fewer innovations (apparently of all ranks) would have resulted from the dissolution of the largest firms.[26] He reports evidence that the exact opposite would have been true in the steel industry, with a weaker indication that little or nothing would have happened to the number of innovations introduced in the other two industries.

[25] Statistical analysis appears to indicate the reasons to be (1) small firms lacked the scale of output to use the innovations profitably, and (2) they lacked the resources to finance and bear the risks of the relatively large investments required by the innovations.

[26] "Size of Firm, Market Structure, and Innovation," *op. cit.,* pp. 565-567.

### Conclusions

In general, the case for bigness and fewness as a stimulus to industry R & D activity appears, on the basis of fairly extensive evidence, to be quite weak. The evidence of the influence of size and concentration on innovation is much more limited, but the influences of these factors appears to be mixed.

Perhaps the most sensible conclusion to be drawn from the foregoing studies is that each industry should be treated as an individual entity. The consistent, but opposite, results obtained in the studies of the effects of size and concentration on R & D and innovation in the petroleum and steel industries bear out the wisdom of this conclusion.

# 5 Invention in the Industrial Research Laboratory

## Inventions: Major or Minor?

In the preceding chapter attention was focused on essentially quantitative aspects of research and development in the large industrial corporations. In the present chapter attention will be centered on the *qualitative* character of R & D in the large industrial laboratories. Specifically, I wish to explore the following hypothesis, based on accumulating evidence: With few exceptions, the large industrial laboratories are likely to be minor sources of major, radically new and commercially or militarily important, inventions; rather, they are likely to be major sources of essentially improvement inventions. Put more precisely, the hypothesis states that the relative share of the large industrial laboratories in minor inventions from all sources is likely to exceed the relative share of these laboratories in major inventions from all sources.

Note that the stress on the relative importance of these laboratories as sources of improvement inventions is not necessarily a denigration of the economic importance of this contribution. The cumulative effect of these improvement inventions can be, and often has been, of substantial importance over long periods of time for advancing technology, investment opportunities, and economic growth. The stress on improvement inventions as the principal product of the research laboratories of the large industrial corporations is meant simply to emphasize that, whatever the importance of their contributions, most of the latter is not likely to involve radically new inventive activity.

I cannot claim originality for this hypothesis. After it suggested itself in the course of my investigations, I discovered that others, some of them in the most unlikely positions,[1] had earlier said much the same thing. But, apart from occasional remarks, I can find no discussions attempting to explain or justify this hypothesis. And because if it is reasonably accurate it has numerous ramifications, I have felt the need to set down an extended analysis of some of the apparently important factors that lend support to the hypothesis.

Evidently, the first person to make a study of the origins of major inventions with a view to ascertaining the role of the large industrial laboratories was W. M. Grosvenor. In 1929, he published the results of a study of seventy-two major inventions made since 1889 in which he found that only twelve of the seventy-two (or 17 percent) originated in corporate laboratories.[2] Into Grosvenor's group fell such inventions as the submarine, the dial telephone, the Diesel engine, moving pictures, calcium carbide, carborundum, and others. Of course, the

---

[1] See particularly the statement quoted below (p. 109) of Dr. Frank Jewett, former President of Bell Laboratories.

[2] W. M. Grosvenor, "The Seeds of Progress," *Chemical Markets* (1929), pp. 23, 24, 26 (cited in H. S. Hatfield, *The Inventor and His World* [Pelican Books, West Drayton, Middlesex, 1948], p. 47). Hatfield cites this article, along with other evidence, in support of a viewpoint virtually the same as the hypothesis set forth above; see Hatfield, pp. 46-50 and *passim*. It is clear that Hatfield, an accomplished scientist in his own right, firmly believes that what was true in the period covered by the Grosvenor study is no less true today. Exploratory talks on this subject that I have had with scientists in various positions indicate ready agreement among them with the hypothesis.

Grosvenor study encompassed a period that preceded the recent explosion of industry spending on research and development, mostly in its own laboratories.

In search of more recent data, let us turn again to the previously mentioned study of inventions headed by Professor Jewkes.[3] This study sought the origins of sixty-one major inventions made exclusively in the twentieth century. Twelve out of the sixty-one major inventions (20 percent) could be attributed to the laboratories of large corporations. These included nylon, the transistor, Freon refrigerants, tetraethyl lead, and Krilium.

To obtain information on the origins of inventions of recent vintage, we may turn again to the present writer's study of twenty-seven major inventions made during the decade 1946-55, inclusive.[4] Of the twenty-seven, seven (26 percent) were the products of large industrial laboratories; these included cold sterilization, terrelac, and Vitamin $B_{12}$. (The remainder came from independent inventors, small firms, an agronomist working more or less by himself in an agricultural experiment station, and three universities.)

The foregoing studies are based on general samples of major inventions.[5] Recently, there have been a number of other stud-

[3] J. Jewkes, D. Sawers, and R. Stillerman, *The Sources of Invention* (London, Macmillan and Co., 1958), particularly pp. 72-88 and Part II. See above, Chapter 1, pp. 16-17.

[4] See p. 16.

[5] None of these studies can be said to be based on random samples of major inventions, in a statistically meaningful sense. The only source of truly random samples would be patent data. But the patent data are very deficient for studies of major inventions because of a proliferation of patents taken by large corporations on marginal variations of original, basic inventions in order to maintain control over earlier patents, create roadblocks for competitors, or avoid the possibility of royalty payments to others at some future time. Moreover, independent inventors are given to much indiscriminate patenting, too. Finally, there is the apparent anomaly that while R & D spending has rocketed, the absolute number of patents taken out in recent years has remained virtually unchanged.

ies of inventions utilizing different approaches. One consists of an examination of the origins of the twenty-five major product and process innovations of E. I. du Pont de Nemours and Company between 1920 and 1950.[6] Out of the eighteen new products, five (almost 28 percent) originated in the research performed in the Du Pont laboratories; a sixth, synthetic methanol, was apparently discovered by Du Pont independently after it had been discovered by an independent French chemist and a German company of undetermined size and almost simultaneously with a small American firm; hence there is some doubt about how this invention should be credited. Also, one of the five Du Pont new products credited to its laboratories, polymeric color film, invented in 1949, has apparently not yet been marketed; so there is a serious question as to whether it should be included. If not, the Du Pont new product list reduces to seventeen, with four (24 percent) unmistakably the results of Du Pont research, and a fifth shared with three others. It may also be noted that of these last four or five new product innovations only three (neoprene, nylon, and orlon) have as yet achieved substantial commercial significance.

In contrast to the rather small proportion of Du Pont new product innovations that originated in the Du Pont laboratories is the large proportion of this company's new product and process improvements for which its laboratories were responsible. Of seven such improvements introduced by Du Pont between 1920 and 1950, five (70 percent) were the result of Du Pont research. Evidently, this famous laboratory has been more successful in improving on discoveries of others than in originating major inventions of its own.

No less interesting is the information that despite a vast in-

[6] W. F. Mueller, "The Origins of the Basic Inventions Underlying Du Pont's Major Product and Process Innovations, 1920-1950," Universities-National Bureau Conference, *The Rate and Direction of Inventive Activity: Economic and Social Factors* (Princeton, Princeton University Press, 1962), p. 323.

crease in its research budget since 1920 (well over thirty-eight-fold), the basic work on two of the three really commercially important product innovations for which the Du Pont laboratories have been responsible (namely, neoprene and nylon) was completed by the late 1920's and early 1930's, when the company's research budgets averaged $5 million annually. And orlon was a direct outgrowth of the researches performed and know-how acquired in connection with the discovery of nylon. Even its greatest successes in product and process improvements, Duco lacquers and moistureproof cellophane, were achieved in the 1920's.[7]

Now let us turn to some specific industry studies. The first of these is a study of the origins of inventions in the American aluminum industry from 1946 to 1957.[8] Five categories of process and product inventions were examined, and the results are highly revealing in a number of respects about the character of inventive activity that goes on in this industry, particularly in the laboratories of the giant producers of primary aluminum.

Of 149 inventions in aluminum welding and fabricating techniques and aluminum finishing, only seventeen originated in the research of the big primary producers; in contrast, seventy-five came from the relatively small and numerous equipment manufacturers. More significantly, perhaps, the large primary producers were responsible for only one out of seven (14 percent) major inventions in these categories, and this one was developed jointly with another firm. Three of the seven were the work of independents.

It is in the invention of end-product applications of aluminum that the big primary producers begin to come into their

[7] *Ibid.*, p. 344.

[8] M. J. Peck, "Inventions in the Post-War American Aluminum Industry," in Universities-National Bureau Conference, *op. cit.*, p. 279.

own. Although "end-product manufacturers are the major source of these inventions, . . . the primary producers are also important contributors."[9] However, whatever inventing is involved in this category is mostly of a very low order (for example, aluminum lifeboats, building products such as store fronts and lighting fixtures, and mine props and beams are representative instances of "invention" in end-product applications of aluminum).

Readers may not be surprised, perhaps, to learn that the big primary producers dominate in the invention of aluminum alloys; between 1946 and 1957 they were responsible for thirty out of thirty-nine such inventions. From the standpoint of commercial importance, however, all these inventions must be ranked as minor in importance, individually and collectively. "New alloys account for only a small fraction of the total sales of aluminum ingot . . . [and] these inventions have apparently played a minor role in the increase in aluminum demand."[10]

Except for this last category, the total invention record of the large aluminum-producing firms is apparently unimpressive. To a considerable extent, however, this fact follows a pattern familiar to students of the aluminum industry. Before World War II, most of the major inventions in this industry originated outside the industry itself. As a matter of fact, in the basic metals industry generally, the large firms have contributed negligibly to the stream of major inventions since the turn of the century. The results of a study conducted by the present writer of thirteen major innovations in the American steel industry between 1940 and 1955 (ten after 1950) indicate that, in this respect, nothing has changed. Of the thirteen, none was based on inventions from American companies, although four

9 *Ibid.*, p. 291.
10 *Ibid.*, p. 292.

came from inventions in European companies. Seven of the thirteen were invented by independent inventors.[11]

In still another industry study, that of the petroleum refining industry, the origins of the major inventions in the refining (cracking) of petroleum were investigated.[12] Here the results may be summarized quite briefly. All seven basic, major inventions underlying past and present refining processes were made by independent inventors, with the big refining companies providing a number of improvements—some quite important, but improvements nonetheless.

Evidence of a rather different sort may also be presented in the form of the results of a statistical analysis of the relation between R & D expenditures, size of firm, and major inventions in the chemical, petroleum, and steel industries over different time intervals.[13] In each of these industries, when the firm's expenditures for R & D were held constant (in a multiple correlation and regression analysis), increases in size of firm were associated with a decline in inventive output. Thus, this evidence suggests that the productivity of an R & D effort of a given scale diminishes as the size of firm increases—at least within the size-range of the firms included in the study.[14]

11 It is also interesting to note that of the six steel innovations that were invented before 1940, three came from companies and one from a solo inventor; but of the seven invented after 1940, six were the results of research of independent inventors, while only one was the result of company-sponsored research. Thus, in this case, at least, there is no trend whatever in the proportion of major inventions originating in company laboratories; in fact, the trend is in exactly the opposite direction.

12 J. L. Enos, "Invention and Innovation in the Petroleum Refining Industry," in Universities-National Bureau Conference, *op. cit.*, p. 299.

13 E. Mansfield, "Industrial Research and Development Expenditures: Determinants, Prospects, and Relation to Size of Firm and Inventive Output," *Journal of Political Economy*, 72 (August 1964), 334-336.

14 It is also interesting to note that not only does the probability that inventions will be significant thus appear to decline as a firm gets bigger, but there is also evidence that larger firms have to spend more to get any kind of invention. This last is suggested by data on R & D expendi-

The foregoing constitutes the brunt of the evidence that has led to the hypothesis that the large industrial laboratories are likely to be minor sources of major inventions but major sources of improvement inventions. This evidence cannot be considered conclusive. With the possible exception of the one on Du Pont, all the invention studies suffer from a lack of any hard and fast criterion for ranking the economic importance of the inventions surveyed. So far as new product inventions are concerned, however, all could seek refuge in the familiar "index number" problem; in other words, given differences in preference functions, and/or an inability in the present state of knowledge to define empirically a community welfare function, it is just about impossible to establish a true ranking of the relative economic importance of inventions. New process and intermediate-product inventions may in principle be evaluated on the basis of some net cost-saving or net addition-to-final-product criteria; but implementation of such criteria for more than a few such inventions would involve well nigh a lifetime's work.

On the plus side of the evidence is consistency of the results. Whatever the criteria of importance employed, all the studies (except the statistical one, which did not report on this point) reveal less than 30 percent of important inventions to be the product of the research laboratories of large companies. And,

---

tures per patent pending by size of firm in six different industry groups (machinery, chemicals, electric equipment, petroleum, instruments, and all other industries) for 1953, the last time such data were collected. Thus, in each industry firms employing more than 5,000 people spent more on R & D per patent than did firms employing less than 1,000 people. In every industry except chemicals, firms in the largest size class spent more on R & D per patent than did firms in the next smaller one (1,000-4,999 employees). For all industries combined, firms employing more than 5,000 people spent about twice as much on R & D per patent as the smaller firms did. See J. Schmookler, "The Size of Firm and the Growth of Knowledge," mimeographed paper presented to the Subcommittee on Antitrust and Monopoly, United States Senate, May 27, 1964.

perhaps most significant, there is not one other study of inventions that provides contrary evidence. With all its faults, therefore, the evidence, if not conclusive, is very suggestive, and it is worthwhile exploring reasons why further evidence may be expected to disclose much the same pattern—in other words, exploring reasons why the hypothesis regarding the character of inventions emanating from the large industrial laboratories is likely to be fairly general.

### Economic Factors

In quest of economic explanations of the foregoing evidence and the hypothesis suggested by the evidence, I have come upon several that for convenience may be grouped into three categories: (1) company aims and objectives in the conduct of their R & D programs; (2) the sources of ideas for these programs and the location of "lab" facilities; and (3) the influence of vested positions. Let us examine each of these in turn.

#### COMPANY R & D AIMS AND OBJECTIVES

Perhaps the most interesting type of economic information to come to light in support of the hypothesis comes from a number of questionnaire and interview studies all pointing to the great emphasis on prompt benefits from the bulk of corporate funds allocated to R & D. In 1958, a McGraw-Hill survey that embraced almost every large company in United States industry and commerce asked: "How soon do you expect your expenditures on research and development to pay off?" [15] Thirty-

[15] See D. M. Keezer, "The Outlook for Expenditures on Research and Development during the Next Decade," *American Economic Review*, 46 (May

nine percent replied that they expected their R & D to pay off in less than three years; another 52 percent indicated an expected payoff in three to five years; 9 percent put the expected payoff at six years or more. In short, 91 percent of the reporting firms expected a payoff from their R & D spending in no more than five years. Since the history of major inventions shows that most of them have taken considerably more time than this before they were even ready for commercial exploitation, the emphasis on the short payoff would seem to indicate that even applied research in most industrial laboratories is geared toward improvements or minor variants of extant products and processes rather than the creation of radically new ones.

Though not as precise as the McGraw-Hill survey, there is other evidence of the tendency of industrial research to stress projects featuring the short payoff. A study of objectives of research programs of almost seven hundred companies made by the National Association of Manufacturers disclosed that 33 percent directed their research toward "immediate benefits," 40 percent toward both "immediate" and "long-term benefits," and 27 percent toward long-term benefits.[16] And all that the Bureau of Labor Statistics could report, after an interview study of two hundred large corporations accounting for more than two thirds of 1953 costs of R & D performance by private industry, was that "at least three-fourths of the companies . . . supported *some* longer term RD projects directed toward

---

1960), 365-366 and *passim*. See also, D. Greenwald, "The Annual McGraw-Hill Research and Development Survey," in National Science Foundation, *Methodology of Statistics on Research and Development* (Washington, D. C., U. S. Government Printing Office, 1959), p. 53. It may be noted that this McGraw-Hill survey, started in 1958, is part of the well-known McGraw-Hill questionnaire on business investment plans.

16 See *Trends in Industrial Research and Patent Practices* (New York, National Association of Manufacturers, 1948), p. 6. See also the remarks of N. A. Shepard in C. C. Furnas, ed., *Research in Industry* (New York, D. Van Nostrand Co., 1948), p. 62.

new products and processes and sometimes to diversification of products." [17]

The McGraw-Hill study referred to above also asked: "What will be the main purpose of your research program?" Forty-one percent of responding firms indicated "improvement in new products"; 48 percent replied "new products" and 11 percent "new processes." [18] Lest the reader interpret the rather large proportion of firms (48 percent) stressing new products as somewhat damaging evidence for the hypothesis, let me remind him of the broad interpretation given "new products" by most firms. Coming forth with another hair spray, or a higher octane gasoline, or another synthetic detergent, a company will call these new products, but these ordinarily involve little that can usefully be described as research. Keezer himself notes that "a large proportion of the outlays on new products occurs in industries, such as food or automobiles, where the proportion of research on such products is small relative to development." [19]

What explanation can be adduced for this apparent emphasis on industry-financed research projects featuring the short payoff? Investigation reveals a multiplicity of forces to be at

[17] National Science Foundation, *Science and Engineering in American Industry* (Washington, D. C., U. S. Government Printing Office, 1956), p. 44. (Italics mine.) What is involved in the distinction between "new products" and "diversification of products" I am unable to determine, unless diversification is meant to be synonymous with improvement.

[18] Keezer, *op. cit.*, p. 365. That the tendency to emphasize short-term projects is not limited to United States industrial research, but is also to be found, at least, in British industry is mentioned frequently in C. F. Carter and B. R. Williams, *Industry and Technical Progress* (London, Oxford University Press, 1957), pp. 52, 82, and *passim*.

[19] *Op. cit.*, p. 365. It is instructive, I think, to cite *Fortune* along the same lines. After noting how much more than other big research-minded companies General Motors spends on R & D, *Fortune* goes on to observe that only a small fraction of General Motors' R & D activities could be called research. See F. Bello, "The World's Greatest Industrial Laboratory," *Fortune*, 61 (November 1958), 224.

work operating with differential effect, depending on the particular industry, the particular firm and its management, the type of research, product and process, and perhaps with the age of the particular laboratory. For one thing, it is apparent that the growth of industrial spending on R & D has to a considerable extent been motivated by the search for another means of achieving product differentiation. Once some firms turn to R & D for this purpose, the pressure is on their competitors to follow suit. The result is a stream of product improvements or "new" products, often of the questionable nature described earlier. In either case, much of the research involved is inevitably defensive in nature, aimed at protecting market positions, and the emphasis is therefore on rush projects that secure immediate benefits. Certainly, this explanation of the quick-payoff type of research crops up repeatedly in interviews with company officials in many industries, including those considered seriously research-conscious, such as the chemical and petroleum industries.

Synonymous with this kind of competition in research, of course, is a high rate of obsolescence, real or imagined, among competing products. In these circumstances the emphasis on quick-payoff research projects can, from another point of view, be explained by a desire for immediate and certain returns from, or conversely, by a reluctance to sink research funds heavily into products, new or improved, exposed to rapid obsolescence. However, the risk premium can enter the research picture in other ways as well. In the case of cost-saving new or improved *process* inventions, or new or improved process inventions that are demand-increasing because of new applications they make possible, the effect on profits often must wait upon wide diffusion that may occupy years. Substantial discounts for time and uncertainty will then tend to push the resources of even large firms toward R & D projects the profits from which are immediate and certain.[20]

The discount for uncertainty enters into the choice of research projects in still another way. In many cases, the more fundamental applied research is, the less certainty there is of a successful outcome, and in the event of success, of an outcome that a firm is equipped to use. There is, for example, a huge gap between an idea for a radically new product or process and successful experimentation in the laboratory; unforeseen problems commonly arise that were not seen in preliminary investigations indicating the invention to be technically feasible. New materials or mechanical parts or tubes or circuits may have to be invented as necessary adjuncts to the basic invention in question. Failure in these and other purely technical aspects is, of course, as much a part of inventive activity as is success, and the premium on uncertainty at this stage is as high as, if not higher than, it is in any other stage of the innovation process, because here the term unknown is often literally true. Those who depict modern science and technology as resting on such a systematic basis that its results are foreordained reveal a naiveté that can be borne only of colossal ignorance.

Similarly, projects surviving the research laboratory may fail in the development stage. "Pilot-plant" production may disclose insuperable problems, or else problems that can be solved only at prohibitive cost. The difficulty may be inherent or due to inadequate technologists. Or the scale of capital investment may turn out to exceed the firm's resources. Frequently, it takes this kind of advanced development to disclose that the indicated saving in costs from a new process would not warrant the outlays involved in switching from the

[20] Cf. Peck, *op. cit.*, p. 293 and *passim.*

extant to the new process; or that the new product represents
a sufficient advance in quality or can be produced and sold
at a sufficiently low price to capture enough of a market to
pay for itself. Of course, the difficult problems of estimating
probable markets, costs, and adequacy of supply of inputs
often arise from the very beginning to confound the prospective innovator, particularly in the case of the more radical
prospective innovations.

Many of these are familiar matters. But they can and should
be adduced in explanation of the stress placed by large corporations on research projects featuring the short payoff, because the product and process improvements or marginally
new products and processes implicit in this type of project are
just the kinds of things that enable the firm to escape most of
these difficulties and uncertainties. In the words of one indus-
trialist: "Pioneering don't pay." That this individual is not
alone in this sentiment is evidenced by the tendency of large
companies to get into new fields by absorbing smaller ones
that have already made substantial technical and commercial
progress and possess the men with know-how.[21]

---

[21] General Electric moved into the electric range and electric clock fields in
this way, as did General Foods in moving into the frozen-food market and
General Motors in becoming the chief producer of diesel-electric locomo-
tives. For a catalogue of a number of similar cases, see T. K. Quinn, *Giant
Business: A Threat to Democracy* (New York, Exposition Press, 1953), pp.
116-117; and M. N. Friedman, *The Research and Development Factor in
Mergers and Acquisitions,* Study No. 16 of Senate Subcommittee on Patents,
Trademarks, and Copyrights (Washington, D. C., U. S. Government Printing
Office, 1958).

It must have occurred to the reader that the high discount for risk imputed to the large companies should apply with even more force to smaller
companies and independent inventors. The latter would surely seem to be
in a much inferior position, from a financial standpoint, in the capacity to
bear the kinds of risks we have been describing. Furthermore, the much
greater financial and technical resources of the large firm enable it to support many more projects than the small firm and independent inventor, with
the result that the large firm is in a much better position to pool the risks
of failure. Why, then, do the small firms and independents apparently con-

In certain industries, it is true, the discounts for uncertainty seem demonstrably lower than in others, and correspondingly greater amounts of corporate funds are channeled into longer-term research projects. Notable in this respect are certain firms in the chemical, petroleum-refining, electronic and electric equipment, and one or two other industries. In part, the reason seems to be associated with the broad scientific base upon which these industries operate. As remarked earlier, when an industry draws upon a fairly well-advanced basic science, the costs of research and development can be expected to be much cheaper than otherwise.[22]

It is apparent, however, that this is only part of the explanation, for coexisting with the research leaders in these industries are firms of comparable size and stature that are research laggards whose programs are "dictated by merchandising needs" and the pressures of immediate competitive requirements. Much seems to depend on the time horizons of top management, their prior experience (whether they have come up from production, sales, or financial departments), their area of collegiate training (scientific, business, technical), and whether the management was inherited or not.[23] In other industries, such as aircraft, certain firms have recently become very research-minded, conducting much long-term applied and

tinue to dominate the field of major inventions? One possible answer may lie in the much stronger desire for safety and security on the part of the bureaucratic officials of large companies as opposed to officials of small companies and the independent inventor. Another answer may lie in the second and third categories of economic explanations as well as the organizational features of large laboratories discussed below. Some of these explanations reflect differences in risk *preferences* that apparently offset differences in financial *capacities* to bear risk. The rest may be described as reflecting differences in other capacities that offset differences in financial capacities.

[22] See Ch. 2, p. 22.

[23] See W. R. Maclaurin, "Technological Progress in Some American Industries," *American Economic Review*, 44 (May 1954), 177-189.

basic research, because the Federal Government has been footing the bill.

This last fact suggests yet another reason for the predominance of quick-payoff projects amid the unsubsidized research performed in the large industrial laboratories. It is well known that the social returns from basic research are apt to exceed the private returns by a considerable margin and, therefore, to be undersupported in the absence of social intervention.[24] To an indeterminate extent, something of the same is likely to be true of fundamental applied research. In contrast, applied research aimed at marginal improvements of existing products and processes is probably just the type where the net social and private returns are apt to be very close, or at least of the type that will enable the firm to capture enough of the gross social revenues to cover, and perhaps more than cover, the comparatively low costs involved in making improvement inventions.

Some students of R & D activity take the optimistic position that the current concentration on short-payoff projects stems from the comparative newness of many of the industrial research laboratories. Because so many of the new laboratories have arisen in response to the competitive pressures discussed earlier, their emphasis is on the defensive type of project aimed at ensuring the short-term survival of the company. Also, their very newness makes such laboratories less appreciative of and, technically speaking, less equipped to perform the more fundamental types of research needed to create original, radically new inventions. And finally, new laboratories often meet with resistance from other, older departments that view this new one with misgivings. In order to overcome this distrust the research department, therefore, must often devote

[24] See, *e.g.*, R. R. Nelson, "The Simple Economics of Basic Scientific Research," *Journal of Political Economy*, 68 (June 1960), 297-306.

itself to trouble-shooting for a while. Then, having gained the confidence of other departments, it may find itself swamped with problems of improving existing products and processes. Not until it has matured and expanded in size can the new laboratory turn its attention to long-range research projects.

There may be a strong element of truth in this sort of diagnosis and prognosis, and there is some evidence to bear it out. But to one person at least it is not convincing, because there are so many large industrial laboratories of long standing that still concentrate almost exclusively on the kinds of research that inevitably lead to improvements of and/or marginal variations on old products and processes.

### SOURCES OF IDEAS FOR RESEARCH PROGRAMS AND LOCATION OF LABORATORIES

A second type of evidence in support of the hypothesis that the large industrial laboratories are likely to be responsible mainly for the improvement types of inventions has to do with the sources of ideas for research projects. As a result of a large number of case studies, Carter and Williams were led to conclude "that most projects originate outside research departments." [25] Other questionnaire and interview studies point to similar conclusions (if not always in the same proportions; in general the more science-based industries seem to have more projects that originate in the research laboratories).[26] Com-

[25] See Carter and Williams, *op. cit.*, pp. 55-56.

[26] See, *e.g.*, C. E. K. Mees and J. A. Leermakers, *The Organization of Industrial Scientific Research* (New York, McGraw-Hill Book Co., 1950), pp. 218-219; and *Evaluating Research and Development*, I. R. Weschler and P. Brown, eds. (Los Angeles, Institute of Industrial Relations, University of California, 1953), p. 20.

pany customers, sales, and production departments appear to be the most frequent sources of projects originating outside the research laboratory. In the nature of things, it seems evident that these outside sources are most likely to offer suggestions that lead to research on improving current products and processes. Customers typically tend to be interested in improvements in materials or equipment presently in use. Unless the sales force is characterized by exceptional technical training, it too will be concerned principally with maintaining or expanding sales of existing products, or at most with providing suggestions for product improvements—perhaps in response to improvements introduced by competitors or perhaps by perceiving a potential market; "merchandising" is the principal concern of sales departments, and this is not the kind of concern that suggests a likely source of radically new ideas. Production departments are also likely to supply problems that require urgent solutions, such as improvement of raw materials or of processes utilizing these materials.

Even when projects originate in research laboratories, recent developments in corporate organization suggest that a preponderance of such projects is likely to be short-term in nature; these same developments also suggest that the influence of customers, sales, and production groups on the allocation of research budgets may be on the increase. The developments I have in mind are the increasing tendencies toward decentralization of corporations. Most commonly, decentralization has been taking the form of a number of operating divisions centered on types or categories of products, with production and sales operations and management concentrated in the divisions and other major functions carried on by corporate executives and staff.

Accompanying this decentralization of corporate activities has been a decentralization of research and development facilities. Although not all have done so, most companies seem to have adopted the practice of attaching most of their laboratory facilities to their operating divisions, even in those instances where a central laboratory has also been established. "In many large companies, a given division may have a large number of labs concerned with different levels of R & D." [27]

The principal reason for decentralizing R & D has been a desire to establish a closer liaison with the operating divisions. "Permitting the . . . divisional laboratories to establish their own programs and their own priorities led to better service to their clients. They could undertake the problems that were of most interest to [the clients], and they could generally get to know the operating problems so that they could anticipate the needs of their clients." [28]

It would be difficult to find more convincing testimony for the assertion that research projects originating in divisional laboratories are likely to be almost exclusively concerned with the current problems of the operating divisions and therefore to be short-term in perspective and emphasizing modifications in materials, processes, and products—in other words, that such inventions as issue from these laboratories should be principally of the improvement variety.[29] Indeed, it is highly

---

[27] A. H. Rubenstein, "Rate of Organizational Change, Corporate Decentralization, and the Constraints on Research and Development in the Firm," a mimeographed paper presented at the Institute of Management Sciences, Chicago, June 1959. I am indebted to this paper for the information upon which much of the argument of the next few paragraphs rests, although I would not impute all the interpretation I have given it to Professor Rubenstein. See also Mees and Leermakers, *op. cit.*, Ch. 7.

[28] Rubenstein, *op. cit.*, p. 7.

[29] Rubenstein and his research group also found, not unexpectedly, that research programs in these circumstances also tend to be less flexible "in terms of the freedom of the researchers to capitalize on the unexpected and follow technical leads that might appear peripheral to the objectives of the particular assigned projects." (*Ibid.*, p. 10). This is an important point in understanding some of the crucial aspects of industrial research activity,

improbable that a division manager would permit anything else. He has usually made his mark in the corporation just by virtue of talents that are the antithesis of those that would enable him to countenance longer-term research projects. "His ability to make decisions and to make money, to get results quickly and at low cost . . . [in short, his] tendency toward the short-run result with the high probability of success . . . is what makes him so valuable to the corporation." [30] And of course, it is inevitable that the division director of research should gear his program to the desires of the division manager, since "he is clearly tied to his divisional management through his R and D budget, the bulk of his work flow, the hierarchical relationships within the division, and his personal career expectations." [31] Needless to say, this chain of influence may be expected to extend down through the kinds of projects selected by the staff of scientific and technical personnel.

Some writers applaud this influence of production and sales and other departments.[32] They argue that close liaison between the research laboratory and such groups are necessary for efficient choice of projects, in the economic sense of reasonably ensuring a choice of projects that, given the firm's technical, financial, and commercial resources and requirements, can be carried through to commercial fruition. In the interest of the *productivity* of the research laboratory (measured by the proportion of its output that is used), it is deemed important that the research laboratory be given adequate information on the sales and production problems of the company and its customers.

---

one on which we shall animadvert at a later point in this chapter; see below, pp. 102-104.

[30] *Ibid.*, p. 12.

[31] *Ibid.*, p. 14.

[32] See, *e.g.*, Carter and Williams, *op. cit.*, pp. 52-53.

From the viewpoint of the criterion of commercial significance and success of the industrial laboratory, which criterion presumably must dominate in any profit-oriented enterprise, there may be a hard core of truth in this attitude. Nevertheless, it seems incontrovertible that emphasis on current production and sales problems of firms will imply corresponding emphasis on short-term research. And most certainly, any company that judges the productivity of its laboratories on the basis of proportion of output used is going to exert overt or implied pressure on its research director(s) to shy away from the kind of research where the results are either technically or commercially highly uncertain—which is to say the kind of research that ordinarily underlies major inventions.

We are not limited to the realm of pure speculation in contemplating the outcome of divisionalized research. In their investigations of over one hundred decentralized companies in a half-dozen industry groups, Rubenstein and his co-workers have found a tendency toward "automatic elimination of certain alternatives as R and D projects, despite their long-run economies: 'they will take too long; forget them;' (and a tendency toward) focusing attention on the quick and sure payoff as a general operating rule, thus ignoring the potential for larger gains over a longer time period." [33]

I do not mean to imply, of course, that this strong movement toward corporate decentralization and divisionalized research forecloses the conduct of longer-range applied or even basic research. Many large companies have retained central laboratories for just this purpose at the same time as they have established division laboratories. But even in these cases, the budget of the central laboratories comprises a relatively minor proportion of the total R & D budget. The cost of R & D performed at the well-known Kodak Research Laboratories, for

[33] *Ibid.*, pp. 16-17.

example, is only 25 percent of the total cost of R & D conducted by Eastman Kodak.[34] This proportion is undoubtedly on the high side for industry as a whole, which has been averaging between 20 and 25 percent for basic and applied research as a proportion of total industrial R & D performance, considering how broad is the interpretation given "basic" and "applied" research in many industries.

Thus, once again, it is difficult to escape the conclusion that despite the vast sums (about $4.5 billion in 1961) that industry itself is supplying for R & D, its main contribution to technical progress will come in the form of improvement inventions.

THE INFLUENCE OF VESTED POSITIONS

The last of the essentially economic reasons why large industrial laboratories are more likely to produce improvement inventions rather than radically new inventions has to do with the nature of the R & D activities of an industrial laboratory that has achieved paramount success. Even such a laboratory tends to focus its research on the products from which financial success has been obtained. If the firm has built up a strong patent position, there are powerful reasons for concentrating its research in areas that will enable it to maintain its patent grip. Patent position aside, however, no firm is likely to be willing to conduct research that will result in the obsolescence of products that are highly profitable and the markets for which may have been painfully built up in the fairly recent past. Instead, such firms are likely to confine their research activities largely to extensions and refinements of the profitable products, that is to improvements within the existing

34 Mees and Leermakers, *op. cit.,* p. 147.

framework, in the interests of consolidation of past gains.

Once more, there is plenty of evidence to bear out this contention. The American automobile industry is a notable case in point. Here is an industry that has possessed a quite satisfactory product with a mass market and heavy capital investment since 1930. As is well known, the research undertaken by the large companies has been aimed principally at engineering improvements of existing products. Even what might be described as *major* improvements have originated outside the research laboratories of the large auto producers. Many, like the new suspension systems, were pioneered by small European concerns, and others, like the automatic transmissions and power steering, were largely the results of the work of independent inventors. In concentrating on features such as greater riding comfort, higher speeds, and a host of minor design changes, none of which required a major new capital investment program, it is clear that the automobile industry has been content to exploit the gains of past success.

Some may argue that the automobile industry never had a serious interest in research; that success was realized without much real research and so there is no reason why it should have suddenly developed one. Damning though this statement is, we can also cite an industry with a strong research propensity, one that was founded on a research conception and leans heavily on developments in basic science for its own commercial advancement. This industry is the electrical equipment industry, dominated in this country by General Electric and Westinghouse. The case in point is the incandescent lamp and the later important invention, the fluorescent lamp. General Electric laboratories were the source of the major advances in the technology of the incandescent lamp between the turn of the century and 1940. As a result of patents thus acquired, General Electric gained virtually complete control of the incandescent lamp industry. Cost reductions through mass production and steady improvement in manufacturing techniques enabled this company to earn large profits from the incandescent lamp. As a result, it was very reluctant to carry on research in fluorescent lighting, a lighting technique that was known as early as 1900 and before. As a matter of fact, by the late 1920's the technology of fluorescent lighting had advanced to the point where this form of lighting was technically possible, and General Electric had the scientists and facilities to bring it to commercial fruition by 1930. It was not until the middle thirties, under the spur of developments in Europe, that the company went to work on the development of the basic model now in general use, although a similar model had been invented in Germany as early as 1926, unknown to General Electric. Even then it was a smaller company, Sylvania Electric, aided by the Justice Department, that broke away from General Electric's lighting monopoly and forced the introduction of the fluorescent lamp in the early 1940's. Also at about this time the last of the basic patents on the incandescent lamp expired.

Here, then, is an excellent example of a research-minded company, wallowing in large profits from an existing product and amply protected by an ironclad patent grip, that sought to avoid the advances in a new lighting technique that would render at least partly obsolete and encroach upon the powerful market position of the successful product. Until forced to change by threats from the outside, it was content to concentrate on improvements in the existing product to protect its entrenched market position.

Nor is this case unique. Commercial television was technologically feasible, with proper financial support, by the early 1930's. But the radio manufacturers, in much the same position as the incandescent lamp manufacturers had been vis à vis the fluorescent lamp, were loath to provide this support while they were still intent on exploiting to the full their investments in radio manufacturing. Other examples could be cited, but I think the foregoing is enough in support of the contention that vested positions in profitable existing products are another economic reason why even successful industrial laboratories may be prone to concentrate their energies and resources in improvement inventions aimed at protecting these vested positions.

Now let us turn to some noneconomic reasons for large industrial laboratories tending to be minor sources of major inventions and major sources of improvement inventions. These latter reasons are primarily organizational in character, and in one person's opinion at least they are potentially just as important as the economic reasons set forth above.

### *Human Factors*

In a nutshell, the argument for organized industrial research is that groups of mediocre (or "average") men, properly equipped with laboratory facilities, can take the place of the creative geniuses of the past. Lest the reader interpret this statement as an exaggeration of current thought, let me quote Mr. Daniel P. Barnard, Research Coordinator of the Standard Oil Company of Indiana: "We find the self-directed individual being largely replaced by highly organized team attack in which we employ many people who, if left entirely to their own devices, might not really be research-minded. In other words, we *hire* people to be curious as a group. We are undertaking to *create* research capability by the sheer pressure of money . . ." [35] In a more restrained vein, the director and assistant director of research at Eastman Kodak Co. have written: "In . . . the planning of research laboratories, . . . all that can be assumed is that it will be possible to obtain, at a fair rate of recompense, well-trained, average men having a taste for research and a certain ability for investigation . . . Men who are only average when dealt with singly may become extremely able by the mental stimulus provided by association with other men working on similar problems." [36]

These views are an extension of the thesis of a number of psychologists and sociologists that in all lines of endeavor the group is superior to the individual. Applied to scientists and technologists, this thesis asserts that the genius, the lone investigator, is passé. The rationale behind the group or team approach to research is deceptively simple and clear: scientific and technical knowledge have grown to such dimensions that it is now impossible to master all relevant fields, and specialization has therefore become unavoidable. But specialization inevitably leads to myopia on the part of the specialist, whose narrow and insular knowledge and capabilities render him increasingly unable to tap the various fields of knowledge needed to produce modern, complicated scientific discoveries and inventions. Team research is the only way out of this dilemma. Teams of experts must be assembled in coordinated fashion to complement each other's specialties, to bring out different points of view, and to select the best of the alternative lines of approach that could have been formulated, in the first place, only *en groupe*.

Essentially, of course, all this is of rather historic vintage. Readers of *New Atlantis* will recall the elaborate lengths to

---

[35] *Proceedings of the Ninth Annual Conference on the Administration of Research* (Northwestern University, September 1955), p. 26 (cited in Jewkes, Sawers and Stillerman, *op. cit.*, p. 240n.).

[36] Mees and Leermakers, *op. cit.*, pp. 207, 208.

which Bacon went to describe arrangements for bringing together specialists from different fields.[37] What the modern advocates of teamwork have done, however, is to take a vehicle basically designed to foster the exchange of information among specialists and convert (or pervert) it into something for which it was never intended, namely, an instrument of creative activity. Groups of specialists can and often do talk together and stimulate each other through an exchange of ideas; but rarely, if ever, do they think together, let alone *create* together.[38] The champions of team research have, in short, exaggerated its advantages and ignored its inherent drawbacks as an agent of original discovery and invention.

We now want to see what the main drawbacks of team research are and how they are likely to be conducive to improvement inventions rather than original creations.

THE INDUSTRIAL LABORATORY AND THE
CREATIVE SCIENTIST AND INVENTOR

In his study of *The Organization Man*, William Whyte cites an investigation by one of his *Fortune* colleagues, Francis Bello, into the caliber of young scientists in the industrial laboratories.[39] Turning first to the foundations and Government agencies such as the Office of Naval Research and Atomic Energy Commission (groups that may be expected to know

37 Jewkes, Sawers, and Stillerman, *op. cit.*, p. 161; also note that Lavoisier advocated the same idea in 1793.

38 Sociologists have gathered evidence indicating that team research of the kind described above actually has a depressing effect on creativity. See H. A. Shepard, *et al.*, *Some Social Attributes of Industrial Research and Development Groups*, Program Report (Cambridge, Mass., Massachusetts Institute of Technology, 1954).

39 William Whyte, *The Organization Man* (Garden City, N. Y., Doubleday & Co., 1956).

who and where the best men are), he asked them to nominate the scientists under forty whom they thought among the most promising. After elimination of duplications, 225 names were obtained. Of this total, only four were found to be in the industrial laboratories. Fearing bias, Bello next went to directors of leading corporate laboratories and university scientists and asked them for nominations of top scientists in industry. Only 35 names were obtained, and there were only seven corporation laboratories in which at least two men were nominated as outstanding and in which one man had at least two votes. "Most industrial scientists, Bello had to conclude, don't know one another, nor are they known by anybody else." [40]

Although this study was concerned with scientists in the strictest meaning of this term, it is fair to presume, on the basis of apparent sources of most major inventions and also on the basis of certain similar mentalities on the part of most creative scientists and inventors, that there is a similar absence of original inventors in the big industrial laboratories. Why? Why, despite the good salaries and security, the elaborate facilities and technical aids, does the creative individual evidently shy away from the industrial laboratory? In answer, we should begin by comparing the characteristics of the typical large corporate research laboratory with the characteristics of the typical creative scientist and inventor.

*The characteristics of the industrial laboratory.* First and foremost, of course, an industrial laboratory represents an effort to *organize* research on the basis of the individual firm's own profit-making criteria. For our purposes, principally involved in this effort is the assembling of a group of scientists and engineers amenable to cooperative or team research on

---

[40] *Ibid.*, p. 228. See also S. Marcson, *The Scientist in American Industry* (New York, Harper and Bros., 1960), p. 54.

problems that the research director and/or other company officials deem relevant by and large to the goals of the firm.

How does the typical firm interpret amenability to team research? In general, this appears to mean normal, well-rounded, company-oriented people.[41] In brief, he must be a loyal organization man whose chief trait must be not his creative capacities, but his abilities to work in consonance with other people and willingness to subordinate personal interests to group interests. *Harmony* is the keynote to successful team research; the ability to come to agreement with colleagues, to see their points of view; a cooperative spirit, a well-adjusted personality—these are the distinctive features of the members of a "successful" research team.

Brilliance is fine—if you can get it in combination with these other traits. But the trouble is that you rarely can. The brilliant scientist and technologist is apt to be erratic and eccentric—an "oddball." Personally, the research director may have nothing against oddballs, but they are ordinarily difficult to accommodate in the smoothly functioning research organization. They tend to be moody, uncooperative, are often focuses of dissension, and as a result they destroy group morale. Organized teams simply cannot tolerate this. And the more highly organized the research program and the greater the stress on team research, the less the brilliant oddball is tolerated, and the more the emphasis is on the ability of the prospective employee to get along with other members of the team and the preservation of harmonious interpersonal relations in the lab-

41 Cf. L. Steele, "Personnel Practices in Industrial Laboratories," *Personnel*, 29 (May 1953), 235; N. Kaplan, "Some Organizational Factors Affecting Creativity," *IRE Transactions on Engineering Management*, Vol. EM-7, (March 1960), 24-29; Mees and Leermakers, *op. cit.*, pp. 207-210; Whyte, *op. cit.*, pp. 231-235; and the discussion of C. P. Haskins in C. C. Furnas (ed.), *op. cit.*, p. 183.

oratory. Occasionally there are industrial research organizations that will put up with an oddball or two in the expectation that his special creative talents will redeem his other drawbacks. But these are the exception. Most research directors are more concerned with the overall efficiency of their laboratories and find it wise to sacrifice the potential contribution of the oddball for the "greater good" of the organization.[42]

Now how does the typical firm interpret the word *relevance* in establishing research programs? Since the firm is above all a profit-making institution, it is commonly held that the task of a research laboratory "is not simply to solve scientific and technological problems, but to solve those problems which are most relevant to the . . . market position of the firm." [43] But who is to decide what lines of research are most relevant and on what basis? Relevance is not easily defined. Until very recently, the cotton textile industry took the position that the definition of its industry was bounded by "cotton textiles," period. Hence it is not surprising that all the present synthetic fibers originated outside this industry. A similarly narrow definition of goals and industry is an important reason for origination of paper substitutes outside the paper pulp industry. The telegraph industry failed to visualize the potential importance of the telephone, and the extremely research-conscious American Bell Telephone and General Electric Companies remained persistently blind to the potentialities of radio; yet in all three cases, the research and development involved by any standards would be described as relevant to the firms' activities.

If research workers are any good, which is to say, creative,

---

[42] A perfect example of this attitude is described in Whyte, *op. cit.*, pp. 234-235.

[43] C. F. Carter and B. R. Williams, *op. cit.*, p. 47. See also Mees and Leermakers, *op. cit.*, Ch. XI, *passim*.

their interests tend to go off on tangents, because their work constantly suggests new ideas and problems. Of course, all research directors will at least acknowledge that warm receptions to new ideas and freedom to choose problems and change directions are important factors in the overall creativeness of a laboratory.[44] But all must "naturally" pass the test of relevance. If the new idea lends impetus to the project, pushes it closer to completion, then it is a fine idea. But if it threatens to sidetrack the project, or to lead it in a different direction, or even to produce answers and results at odds with those expected and in new areas, then the new idea may not be so fine.

Who finally decides? Generally, the director of the laboratory marks out the areas of research and selects the projects to be undertaken, sometimes in consultation with senior members of his staff, and now with increasing frequency in consultation with top management, usually a committee. "Probably the most important principle [in the selection of the laboratory program] is . . . the research director's judgment . . . he must decide what investigations should be undertaken and in what directions manpower should be applied . . . it is his responsibility to select and approve the individual problems and programs and to place them in the proper order of their importance." [45] How he decides usually depends on his particular interests and his conception of the scope of the com-

---

44 See Kaplan, *op. cit., passim;* see also, the interesting discussion by Marcson, *op. cit.,* pp. 112-114.

45 Mees and Leermakers, *op. cit.,* pp. 212 and 232. See also, Marcson, *op. cit.,* pp. 42-43; N. A. Shepard, in C. C. Furnas (ed.), *op. cit.,* pp. 60-61; R. R. Nelson, "The Economics of Invention: A Survey of the Literature," *The Journal of Business,* 32 (April 1959), 124-125; L. W. Steele, "The Challenge of Research Management," *Industrial and Engineering Chemistry,* 17 (November 1957), p. 114A; and H. A. Shepard, "The Destructive Side of Creativity," *Industrial and Engineering Chemistry,* 7 (September 1957), 109A, 110A.

pany's commercial interests, as well as on the more specific or practical problems concerning budgets, types and quality of personnel and personnel policies, and so forth.

Thus, with some exceptions, the control of most industrial laboratories tends to be rather centralized, with early programming by the director of research in which each worker is assigned a prearranged task. Although research directors will typically stress freedom of action on the part of their scientists and technologists as important for creativity,[46] it is clear that they are "committed to a concept of *limited* creativity at best. That is, they . . . encourage creative ideas within fairly restricted limits of programs and projects and goals of the research organization." [47]

*The characteristics of the creative scientist and inventor.* Whatever the desires of the team-oriented research laboratory, they are not likely to be fulfilled by the typical creative scientist and inventor. If there is a dominant trait marking such persons, it is their fierce independence, a fact noted uniformly by virtually every study of the personalities of creative technical people. In their work they insist on following their own interests, at their discretion, without direction or interference. Rejection of accepted routine and convention, rebellion against classical modes of thought, repudiation of the tried and true and of expert authority, insistence on going "where angels

[46] Dr. Mees, of Eastman Kodak, whom we quoted earlier on the central role of the research director, and who is, to say the least, ambivalent on the subject of the freedom to be allowed the research worker, has poignantly said: "The best person to decide what research work shall be done is the man who is doing the research. The next best is the head of the department. After that you leave the field of best persons and meet increasingly worse groups. The first of these is the research director, who is probably wrong more than half of the time. Then comes a committee, which is wrong most of the time. Finally, there is a committee of company vice presidents, which is wrong all of the time." See C. E. K. Mees, *The Path of Science* (New York, John Wiley & Sons, 1946), p. 135.

[47] Kaplan, *op. cit.*, p. 29; see also, Marcson, *op. cit.*, pp. 26, 104-105.

fear to tread"—these are the persistent characteristics of the creative scientist and inventor. Monomania, the idée fixe, and the refusal to be deterred by apparently insurmountable difficulties, are part of the same mold.[48]

Typically, the creative scientist or inventor balks at routine. In the grips of his own inner compulsions, eager to get on with his work, he works at odd hours and all hours. The idea of a steady round of nine-to-five work, with an hour off for lunch, is ordinarily anathema. Creative work just does not fit routine; the flow of ideas simply does not follow the clock; it is impossible to start and stop thinking on arbitrary time schedules. A man in the midst of creative activity is a man completely absorbed; he works to the temporary exclusion of all other considerations until success has been achieved. Once again, study after study of successful inventors all seem to concur on this trait, and anyone who has ever engaged in creative work will readily comprehend it.

Commonly, the creative scientist and inventor work alone (or at best with ancillary aids only), by personal choice or otherwise. It is this characteristic that is responsible, of course, for the appellation of lone-wolf inventor. This term is often misinterpreted, however. It is not the physical isolation as such that is significant, but the intellectual isolation. This is not to say that the lone-wolf inventor is cut off from the mainstream of ideas, though he sometimes is. Rather, it is that at heart he

[48] Jewkes, Sawers, and Stillerman, *op. cit.*, p. 117, tell how Farnsworth, one of television's pioneers, achieved success after a professor had given four good reasons why his ideas were doomed to failure; how the success of short-wave radio in long-range transmission was attained after formal proof by mathematicians that this was impossible; how the inventor of xerography achieved success in the face of scorn of his efforts by his technical friends, etc. See also, Marcson, *op. cit.*, pp. 18-19; Steele, *op. cit.*, pp. 109A-110A; C. D. Flory, "Developing and Using Creative Abilities," *Chemical Engineering Progress*, 49 (December 1953), 678; and O. Z. Ohmann, "The Care and Feeding of the Creative Center—the Inventor," *Chemical Engineering Progress*, 53 (April 1957), 22.

is a rebel, a faultfinder, a stubborn questioner—in short, an intellectual iconoclast. He is set apart because he is challenging accepted ideas or ways of doing things as either deficient or wrong.[49] As much as anything else, this characteristic tends to make him unamenable to, and in the eyes of research directors unsuitable for, organized research.

## THE CLASH OF TRAITS

The distinctive features of the typical industrial laboratory and the creative scientist and inventor we have just described place these two squarely in conflict with one another. As we have seen, the function of the research laboratory and its administrators is to *organize;* the directors of research must be the ones to decide what is to be researched and when. No matter how strong the urge of the scientist and technologist to follow *his* own bent, in *his* own way, and when *he* wants to, with few exceptions the research director cannot permit it; to do so would make a shambles of the organization, and to allow this would be tantamount to denial of the organization's and the director's *raison d'être.*

Not only must the director of research be primarily concerned with the smooth, undisturbed, and continuing functioning of his teams—the "organization"—but he is bound to keep his research program geared or "relevant" to fields deemed most profitable to the firm. However, "it will only be by chance that the almost irresistible lure of intellectual and inventive interest will coincide with the best judgments of what will most profit the firm . . . If the firm, by reference to its own criteria of profit-making, seeks to impose control from outside it runs

[49] Cf. the statement of C. F. Kettering, quoted in C. C. Furnas (ed.), *op. cit.,* pp. 204-205.

the danger of checking the exercise of the very powers it set out to foster," [50] and of frightening off the talents it may—or should—wish to attract.

Both of these dangers seem to have been realized. The Bello study on the conspicuous lack of first-rate scientists in the industrial research laboratories and the evident failure of these laboratories to be responsible for more than a minor proportion of major inventions both testify amply that the creative scientist and inventor have shied away from these organizations. And it is small wonder, given the almost inevitable clash of interests and goals.

Nor are we limited to guesswork about the repressive effects on such talents as the industrial research laboratory is able to attract. In an effort to stimulate creativity, many laboratories have adopted the procedure of permitting their research workers "free time." In general, this means that the research worker can spend part of the company's time (usually between 5 and 10 percent, but sometimes more), facilities, and even money, on work hypothetically of his own choosing. Yet it is a common complaint of research directors that few men are willing to take advantage of the offer and that little originality and imagination seem to be displayed when they do. "Practically all who are now Ph. D.'s," Whyte quotes one research director, "want to be told what to do. They seem to be scared to death to think up problems of their own." [51]

---

[50] Jewkes, Sawers, and Stillerman, *op. cit.*, p. 134; see also, Marcson, *op. cit.*, Chapter 9, *passim*; O. A. Ohmann, *op. cit.*, p. 22; and H. A. Shepard, "Nine Dilemmas in Industrial Research," *Administrative Science Quarterly*, 1 (December 1956), 296-299 and 300-301.

[51] Whyte, *op. cit.*, p. 236. See also N. Kaplan, "The Relation of Creativity to Sociological Variables in Research Organizations," in C. W. Taylor, ed., *Research Conference on the Identification of Creative Scientific Talent* (Salt Lake City, University of Utah Press, 1959), pp. 237-238. Kaplan also notes (p. 239) that the rewards usually go to researchers who use their free time to come up with practical ideas, and not unexpectedly "practicality" turns

This information should occasion no surprise. "A company cannot bring in young men and spend several years to make them into one kind of person, and then expect them, on signal, to be another kind . . . If it indoctrinates them in the bureaucratic skills and asks them to keep their minds on the practical (or relevant), it cannot suddenly stage a sort of creative play period and then, on signal, expect them to be somebody else." [52] Alternatively, of course, the lack of interest in creative work on the part of industrial scientific and technical personnel may reflect not so much the smothering but the screening and repelling of creative talent by the industrial laboratories. If the emphasis in the hiring of personnel is on "average, well-adjusted, team" personalities, to the virtual exclusion of the egomaniacal brilliant ones, and if the latter also find organized research anathema, we should hardly expect to find much creative talent in the industrial laboratories.

Moreover, there is something absurd about this effort at allotment of 5-10 percent of the researcher's paid time in the hope that something really creative will be forthcoming or that the creative person's desire for freedom will thus be appeased. The practice reveals a frightful lack of understanding of the creative process. Creativeness or inventiveness is not something that can be turned off and on here and there. When the flash of inspiration strikes, the typical inventor pursues it for all it is worth. It is well nigh inconceivable to ask him to devote 90-95 percent of his time to company work and fit his own work into an occasional hour a few afternoons a week—

---

out to be defined in terms of the goals and research program of the organization. Whyte, p. 231, has a fine illustration of this same point from Standard Oil of New Jersey. See also N. A. Shepard, *op. cit.*, p. 59; and C. D. Ahlberg and J. C. Honey, *Some Administrative Problems in Government Research* (Washington, D. C., Syracuse University, Washington Research Office, 1951), p. 75.

52 Whyte, *op. cit.*, pp. 236-237.

and at the same time maintain his mental equilibrium and creative urge. Either the idea will wither, or he will go mad from frustration, or he will simply up and quit!

Even laboratories that have tried their best to create an atmosphere typical of the universities by giving some of their better researchers broad freedom in the selection and conduct of projects have found it difficult to attract and *hold* first-rate talent. There are numerous cases on record of top-rank scientists being lured away from universities to such industrial laboratories. But sooner or later most of them leave. They do so not because of any overt pressure to produce quick results but because in the nature of things, in the fact that they are working for profit-oriented institutions, it is impossible to escape the ever-lurking, if covert and implied, pressure to do something useful for the company.

THE LIMITATIONS OF TEAM RESEARCH

Aside from the absence of creative personnel among most teams of organized researchers because of their mutual incompatibility, it is important to recognize the inherent drawbacks of team research per se as a source of major inventions. The essence of team research is, of course, cooperation; cooperation, in turn, implies agreement. And in the urge to reach agreement—on ideas, approaches, techniques, and even on the nature of the problems to be researched—lies one of the severest defects of team research. When groups are forced to reach agreement as a basis for action, the pressure to compromise is continuously at work. Compromise poses the danger of agreeing on what is least objectionable, not what may be most effective and creative. The strong impulse toward consensus means that agreement will tend to center on what the team finds acceptable as common ground. The tendency will therefore be to follow established ideas and methods, the tried and true. Inspirational hunches, novel but vague intuitions are given short shrift when they cannot be spelled out to the satisfaction of all members of the team. Disagreements that threaten interminable squabbles and therefore the productivity of the team are met by decisions to try something else, or delay, or even do nothing at all along particular lines. Botched-up compromises may miss the virtues of the original proposals. At the same time, the most fertile ideas are usually the most novel; they are likely to be the very ones that transcend the familiar, the accepted, the tried and true. Thus they are the most likely candidates for sources of dissension and disagreement. If this is true, then it also follows that they are also most likely to be passed over in favor of more traditional, less novel proposals on which agreement is easier to reach.

THE RESEARCH COMMITTEE

Almost every large company with a reasonably extensive research program has a research coordinating or operating committee.[53] Such committees are variously composed of the heads of the research, sales, production, and finance departments or divisions. Their function? To plan and review the company's research program and budget. Their purpose? To secure "the active support of qualified operating groups and executive officers [and to coordinate] the policies of the various corporate divisions, often with conflicting interests . . . At least there will be no concerted effort against the [research project], since everyone is committed on the advisability of the enter-

[53] See, *e.g.*, the report by C. G. Harrel in C. C. Furnas (ed.), *op. cit.*, pp. 124-127.

prise." [54] Often, when matters of difficult technology are involved, there is a proliferation of subcommittees or panels consisting of specialized technologists from different parts of the company. These subcommittees are justified because information on these problems coming from the research department alone "does not represent the corporation as a unit." [55]

As strong as the urge is on the research teams to reach agreeable compromises, to follow the paths of least resistance, it must be even stronger on company-wide committees to reach agreement on a research program. At the least, the members of laboratories' research teams represent the same department and their interests are centered on science and technology.[56] The company research committees suffer the twofold defect (from the viewpoint of readiness to select bold, new research projects) of being composed primarily of administrators and of representing potentially conflicting interests. Research programs must be balanced in terms of the needs or claims of the operating divisions. Finance officers, typically begrudging and myopic about research expenditures generally, must be appeased and persuaded. Competing views about differences in marketing potentials must be reconciled. In fact, "reconciliation of differences in point of view" among the various organizational units is a key phrase and the distinctive feature of company research committees.

Similarly, a distinctive feature of every administrator is a desire for peace and harmony. He tries to avoid anything disruptive; after all, his reputation as an administrator rests

---

[54] P. D. Foote, director of research in the Gulf Oil Corporation, quoted in Mees and Leermakers, *op. cit.*, pp. 172-174.

[55] *Ibid.*, pp. 173-174.

[56] Even this point can be exaggerated. Where laboratories are decentralized and associated with operating divisions, conflicts arise that are often extra-scientific. And of course, there may be conflicts over allocations of resources even in a centralized laboratory.

heavily on the smoothness with which his organization runs. Personal frictions are the bane of his existence. He is likely to have risen to his position, not only by virtue of his ability, but also by his display of tact and his apparent talents as a good team man, one who has always kept the organization's interests to the fore. Place a group of such administrators on a company research committee and you must expect their behavior to be true to form. Their first and strongest impulse is to seek common ground for agreement, to avoid anything that is divisive. A bold and imaginative, really new idea for research is by its nature divisive; it is inherently unorthodox; as a result, the committee of administrators is apt to be instinctively hostile to it. Bent as they are on reaching amicable agreement, the administrators will tend to concentrate on the obvious, the marginal, for it is in this area that consensus is most easily achieved. The obvious and marginal research projects are, of course, just those that are basically *improvement* types of research.

We have been describing a model or pattern of research organization that, with expected degrees of variation, represents the commonality of industrial laboratories in most of our large corporations. Normally, their personnel consists of mediocre people chosen more for their ability to work well with other people than for their creative talents. The brilliant virtuoso performer is usually considered unqualified because by nature he is not a team man. Equally important, the creative scientist and technologist avoids employment in the industrial laboratories for the very same reasons and also because he generally insists on a degree of independence of thought and action that is incompatible with the centralized control and narrowly oriented goals or profit criteria of most industrial laboratories. Add to these drawbacks the tendencies of the teams that perform the research and the company committees that frequently select the research with an eye to avoiding the disruptive and the unorthodox to reach harmonious agreement. Individually and in combination, these organizational features of industrial research certainly suggest a strong tendency to confine it to conventional investigations into relatively superficial and simple types of problems, problems whose solution is readily anticipated and comparatively inexpensive to obtain. Inevitably, then, the emphasis will be on research projects designed to improve existing products and processes.[57]

Of course, we do occasionally find industrial laboratories that by any criteria must be described as creative, and continually so. The laboratories of the American Telephone and Telegraph and of the General Electric companies are the best and the commonly cited examples. They have apparently been consistently able to overcome the handicaps of the large industrial laboratory we have described. They have been equally able to attract, if not always hold, such topnotch research people as Steinmetz and Langmuir, and Shockley and Brattain.

On the whole, however, the creative industrial laboratories appear to be isolated exceptions. In this connection, it is worthwhile to quote Dr. Frank B. Jewett, former President of the preeminent Bell Laboratories: "I think that it is inevitable that the great bulk of what you might call the run-of-the-mine patents in an industry like ours will inevitably come from your

---

[57] Even when they set out to invent something radically new, the inhibiting influences seem to be at work in the large industrial laboratories. Untold sums were spent by the oil industry before an independent inventor came up with the first commercially feasible process for the catalytic process of petroleum; large sums were also spent in the automobile industry in quest of simple change devices before an independent inventor brought forth the synchromesh; and most recently, an Alaskan boy of seventeen has invented a wheelless car that will float in the air, accomplishing what the laboratories of Curtiss-Wright Corporation could not achieve after spending upwards of a half-million dollars.

own people . . . I think it is equally the case that those few fundamental patents, the things that really mark big changes in the art, are more likely to come from outside than from the inside." [58]

### Conclusions

As was stated at the outset, the cumulative effect of these "run-of-the-mine patents" or improvement inventions, by advancing the state of the arts and promoting investment opportunities and economic growth, can be of substantial importance to society. And from the individual firm's standpoint, the often expensive industrial laboratories may well justify their existence by acting as information monitors and funnels for work done elsewhere and by providing the basis for further development work and adaptation to their companies' specific needs; in this way the product and process improvements needed to maintain and/or advance the firm's market position can be made.

Nevertheless, the "few fundamental patents" are the grist for the improvements; it is the basic inventions that maintain the broad stream of technological progress in the long run. If, for reasons set forth above, the industrial laboratories are apt to be minor sources of major inventions, as they evidently have been, it is important for the future stream of technological progress that this be made clear to a public and public officials that apparently think otherwise. Right now there is a

---

[58] Temporary National Economic Committee, *Hearings on Concentration of Economic Power*, Part I (Washington, D.C., U.S. Government Printing Office, 1939), p. 971. See also the very similar remarks by Ohmann, *op. cit.*, p. 21 (Ohmann is an executive of Standard Oil of Ohio) ; and Quinn, *op. cit.*, Ch. 12 (Quinn was a top-ranking Vice President of General Electric and slated to become President at the time of his resignation).

glib tendency to identify the large industrial laboratories as the source of our major inventive activity, contrary to fact.[59] By itself, this perversion of reality might be harmless. But unfortunately, it has come to be reflected in private and public policies.

In some cases by design, in others by administrative expediency, policies bearing on the inventive process have had the effect of promoting the institutionalization of invention in the large industrial laboratories. Implicitly or explicitly, these policies assume that large teams of organized scientists and technicians working under close administrative guidance, with their tasks and goals carefully preestablished, are indeed the best approach to invention. But it certainly remains to be demonstrated that there is a definite correlation between size of research organization and quality as well as quantity of inventive achievement. On the contrary, the evidence indicates the absence of any such correlation, and the explanations of the evidence set forth in this chapter suggest that there are inherent incompatibilities between the large industrial laboratories and high-level inventive achievement.

Yet without any careful consideration, the laboratories of the large industrial corporations have been receiving all the accolades and most of the support. Although it appears that the bulk of major inventions originate outside these laboratories, particularly in the work of independent inventors and small-

[59] The patent data (discussed earlier, p. 17) provide additional evidence on just how contrary to fact: In recent years, corporations have been taking out roughly 60 percent of total patents in the United States, and independent inventors some 40 percent. At the same time, it appears that of the 60 percent issued to corporations, two thirds come from the industrial laboratories and the rest from corporation employees working outside the laboratories. Hence some 40 percent of the patents issued to corporations originate in organized laboratory research, a figure that just matches the number of patents issued to independent inventors. It may or may not also be significant that 75 percent of patents issued to small companies are commercially used, compared to a 50 percent use rate among patents issued to large companies.

and medium-sized firms, these sources have been relatively neglected and their potential contributions virtually ignored, at least in our formal policies. It seems clear that future efforts to foster technological progress must cease this neglect and develop ways of supporting these wellsprings of fundamental advances in the arts.

**Part 3** | *Research and Development in the Firm: The R & D Budget and Its Allocation*

# 6 Determinants of Research and Development by the Firm

Despite the rapid growth in the volume of R & D conducted in private industry, surprisingly little has been done to investigate statistically the determinants of and the differences in the scale of R & D activity among firms. This chapter represents a report of the results of a study designed to remedy this deficiency, at least in part.

Specifically, we present the results of a least-squares multivariate, cross-section analysis of a number of determinants of R & D activity of 405 firms in twenty-one manufacturing industry groups in the United States for the year 1960. With private industry playing an important and increasing part in the invention process through its large and growing spending on R & D, it behooves us to shed some empirically founded light upon the influences on industrial R & D.

## Hypotheses

The literature on research and development has variously stressed a number of variables as exerting an influence on industrial R & D decisions. On the basis of this discussion, plus a priori considerations and a dash of economic theory, six variables have been selected for inclusion in our statistical model as predictors of industrial R & D activity. The hypotheses underlying their inclusion are presented below.

Before this, however, attention should be called to a variable that is undoubtedly of some importance as an influence on the volume of R & D by the firm, as shown previously,[1] but that has been deliberately excluded from the present model. This variable is size of firm, however measured. The reasons for omitting this variable, most of which are discussed below in connection with the statistical aspects of our model, are many. Here it is sufficient to note that one of the reasons is that the influence of size gives evidence of being strong enough to pose the real threat of swamping almost any other influence. To avoid this danger, and for other reasons, too, it seemed best to handle the size variable in the manner discussed below. Bearing this in mind, we may now proceed with the discussion of the variables included in the model.


SALES


On the basis of interview studies, it is evident that sales, current or immediate past, play an important role in determining the level of R & D activity of many firms. Certainly, this role is not unexpected. Economic theory would bear out the importance of sales to a firm that had any pretensions to being a profit maximizer. Profits are a residual function of sales. In contemplating an expenditure on R & D, a firm may be expected to make some sort of forecast of future revenues

---

[1] See above, pp. 49-56. However, this remark applies only to the absolute amount of R & D performed by the firm, not to the relative amount.

and costs associated with the results of the R & D over the expected lifetime of these results. Expected future receipts minus expected future expenses, properly discounted to the present, will show the expected future gain to be realized on the contemplated R & D expenditure. The decision to incur this expenditure will hinge upon a comparison between its size and the anticipated gain.

At the same time, the future is filled with uncertainty. Hence there is a strong temptation to gauge future sales and profitability by projecting current or immediately past sales into the future. The procedure smacks of certainty and simplicity in a highly uncertain world.

All this indicates that R & D should tend to be positively associated with sales, and the suggestion of such association does recur in numerous interviews.[2] The relation is apparently by no means rigid. In some cases it is reported that an established ratio of R & D to sales represents a maximum amount that the company can afford to spend on R & D. In other cases these ratios are said to represent rough guides in determining R & D budgets: past ratios represent guides to orders of magnitude, rather than fixed ceilings on R & D spending.

However, it is by no means certain that the association between R & D and sales must be positive. For an enterprising management a shrinkage of sales, or perhaps a retardation in their growth, could be a signal to increase R & D spending in an effort to recover lost ground and start sales trends upwards again. Management has frequently stressed the defensive character of its R & D spending, a fact that would seem to be in consonance with a negative relation between R & D and sales. In addition, the fact that the bulk of R & D activity is evidently

[2] On this and other points discussed below, see particularly National Science Foundation, *Science and Engineering in American Industry* (Washington, D. C., U.S. Government Printing Office, 1956), pp. 43-48.

devoted to improvements of existing products and processes aimed at protecting market positions[3] suggests the possibility of a negative relation.

There is nothing in economic theory either that would deny that such a negative relation is consistent with profit maximization. As a matter of fact, we may construct a simple model of the firm to see under what conditions a positive or a negative relation is consistent with profit-maximization. To do so, we begin by writing the following profit function:

$$(1) \qquad F(q,s) = R(q,s) - O(q) - C(s)$$

where

$R(q,s) =$ total revenue as a function of sales, $q$, and R & D, denoted by $s$, which is introduced into the revenue function as a shift parameter, following the convention made familiar by Samuelson.[4]

$O(q) =$ cost of producing and selling each amount of sales.
$C(s) =$ cost as a function of the scale of R & D.

Apart from treating the influence of R & D in a manner analagous to that of, say, advertising expenditures, equation (1) is a fairly conventional construction.

In order for profits to be a maximum, it is necessary that

$$(2) \qquad F_q = R_q - O'(q) = 0$$

$$(3) \qquad F_s =: R_s - C'(s) = 0$$

---

[3] On this, see p. 77 ff.; also W. S. Comanor, "Research and Competitive Product Differentiation in the Pharmaceutical Industry in the United States," *Economica*, 31 (November 1964), pp. 378, 381-382. The importance of improvement inventions should also go far toward erasing doubts of the wisdom of using current or past sales of *old* products as a basis for estimating sales of the apparently *new* ones that originate in R & D; most of the results of R & D are just not that new, being mainly in the nature of differentiated old ones.

[4] See P. A. Samuelson, *Foundations of Economic Analysis* (Cambridge, Mass., Harvard University Press, 1948), p. 17 and *passim*.

(4) $$F_{qq} = R_{qq} - O''(q) < 0$$

(5) $$F_{ss} = R_{ss} - C''(s) < 0$$

(6) $$F_{qq}F_{ss} > (F_{qs})^2$$

Equations (2)–(6) are the usual first- and second-order maximum conditions for a profits function in two variables.

Now our problem is to determine how our firm will vary its R & D in response to a change in sales. Specifically, we wish to know the sign of $ds/dq$: under what conditions will this sign be positive and under what conditions negative? As a profit maximizer, our firm will make any changes in such a way as to continue to satisfy equations (2) and (3). To ascertain the effects of a change in sales on R & D (or for that matter, the effects of a change in R & D on sales), we may allow both variables to vary simultaneously. This is done by differentiating equations (2) and (3) totally[5]:

(7) $$R_{qq}dq + R_{qs}ds - O''(q)dq = 0$$

(8) $$R_{sq}dq + R_{ss}ds - C''(s)\,ds = 0$$

Grouping terms and setting equations (7) and (8) equal to each other (since they are equal to the same thing), we get

(9) $$[R_{qq} - O''(q) - R_{sq}]dq = [R_{ss} - C''(s) - R_{qs}]ds$$

or

(10) $$\frac{ds}{dq} = \frac{R_{qq} - O''(q) - R_{sq}}{R_{ss} - C''(s) - R_{qs}}$$

[5] This technique is standard in the theory of the firm and consumer behavior. See, *e.g.*, Samuelson, *op. cit.*, p. 101, and J. M. Henderson and R. E. Quandt, *Microeconomic Theory* (New York, McGraw-Hill Book Co., 1958), p. 25 ff. and *passim*. Note that equations (7) and (8) each equal zero because of the absence of a budget constraint.

Now, from expressions (4) and (5), $R_{qq} - O''(q) = F_{qq} < 0$, and $R_{ss} - C''(s) = F_{ss} < 0$. Therefore, we can rewrite equation (10) as

(10a)
$$\frac{ds}{dq} = \frac{-F_{qq} - R_{sq}}{-F_{ss} - R_{qs}}$$

Further, if, as is customary, we take equation (1) to be a continuous function, then (by Young's Theorem) the second-order, mixed derivatives are equal, that is, $R_{sq} = R_{qs}$. Immediately, it becomes clear that the sufficient condition for $ds/dq > 0$ is that $R_{sq} (= R_{qs}) \geqslant 0$.

But let us pause to consider the economic content of $R_{sq}$. By definition, $R_{sq} \equiv \partial(\partial R/\partial q)/\partial s$. Since $\partial R/\partial q$ is, simply, marginal revenue, the question of the sign of $R_{sq}$ is the question of the behavior of the marginal revenue function in response to a change in R & D. In turn, this question is nothing but the effect on the elasticity of the demand function of a change in R & D. As we remarked earlier, the evidence is strong that by far most industrial R & D has been motivated by the search for achieving another means of product differentiation—sometimes as an alternative but probably more often in addition to advertising. It is often said that the primary goal of advertising is to shift the firm's demand function to the right *and to make it less elastic*. To say the least, therefore, it is equally possible that $R_{sq}(= R_{qs}) < 0$. In this case equation (10a) appears as

(10b)
$$\frac{ds}{dq} = \frac{-F_{qq} + R_{sq}}{-F_{ss} + R_{qs}}$$

Still, examination of (10b) reveals that although $R_{sq} < 0$ is a necessary condition for $ds/dq < 0$, it is not a sufficient condition. Thus, if $|F_{qq}| > |R_{sq}|$ and $|F_{ss}| > |R_{sq}|$, *or* $|F_{qq}| < |R_{sq}|$ and $|F_{ss}| < |R_{sq}|$, $ds/dq > 0$. In short, the necessary and sufficient conditions for $ds/dq < 0$ are $R_{sq} < 0$, $|F_{qq}| > |R_{sq}|$ and

$|F_{ss}| < |R_{sq}|$, *or* $R_{sq} < 0$, $|F_{qq}| < |R_{sq}|$ and $|F_{ss}| > |R_{sq}|$. Going one step further we can observe, again from equations (4) and (5), that $R_{sq} = F_{sq}$ and $R_{qs} = F_{qs}$. Consequently, whether or not $ds/dq < 0$ when $R_{sq} = F_{sq} = R_{qs} = F_{qs} < 0$ depends on the absolute values of the second-order pure and mixed partial derivatives of the profits function.

This appears to be as far as our mathematics and economics will take us. Suffice it to note that on the face of things there does not seem to be anything implausible about the conditions for $ds/dq < 0$ in our model. Hence we may conclude, both on the basis of intuition and a bit of economic theory, that the sign of the coefficient of a sales variable in an R & D regression model could be *either* positive *or* negative.

## PROFITS

It may well be that profits, rather than sales, play an important role in determining the scale of R & D by the firm. The firms whose behavior with respect to R & D we are trying to describe do operate within the environs of a profits system. Profits are indeed perhaps the prime mover in a private enterprise economy. Hence all that we have said above about the possible relations between sales and R & D may apply equally to profits and R & D.

Thus when profits (current or immediate past) are high, firms may expand their R & D activities and contract them when profits are low. In either case, the firm would be using recent profits as a seemingly concrete indicator of future profitability of R & D activities. Or conversely, as with sales, a firm may view falling profits or losses as an indicator to expand R & D in an effort to recoup.

From a pragmatic standpoint, there is little to choose between sales and profits as an indicator of future profitability in a regression model of R & D. For this reason, and for another to be discussed, it was decided to experiment with both variables in our regression model.

## LIQUIDITY VARIABLES: PROFITS AND DEPRECIATION

Profits can function not only as an indicator of future profitability but also, in the form of retained earnings, as a source of finance. It is commonly held that adequate funds must be available to finance R & D programs themselves and to permit optimum utilization of research findings. The latter is no less important than the former in the present study, for exploitation of research findings is clearly one of the prerequisites to maintenance and expansion of R & D programs. At the same time, and for well-known reasons, firms are likely to be unwilling or unable to finance R & D programs by tapping outside sources of funds; the same is true of the investments necessary to exploit commercially the results therefrom. Hence, it seems reasonable to hypothesize that the availability of internal sources of funds should tend to play a significant role among the determinants of the scale of a firm's R & D activities.

However, even though profits may act in a capacity different from that assigned to them earlier and different from the role assigned to sales, a serious problem arises in any effort to include them in the same regression model along with sales. The one being a residual of the other, profits and sales are subject to common influences. As such they cannot be considered independent explanatory variables in the same regression model. This problem of multicollinearity makes it necessary to analyze the influences of sales and profits separately, in a manner described below.

At the same time, internal sources of funds consist not only of retained earnings but also depreciation allowances. Consequently, a separate variable for this internal source of finance was included in our regression model.

So far as expected sign is concerned, our hypothesis with respect to finance variables dictates the expectation that the sign of the coefficient of the depreciation variable should be positive. And to the extent that the profits variable functions as a finance influence, the same sign may be expected with respect to the coefficient of this variable. However, a statistically significant coefficient possessing a minus sign need not, in and of itself, indicate the probable falsity of the finance hypothesis, for it may indicate that profits are functioning in the possible alternative role assigned this variable, namely, as a signal for the firm to bestir itself by way of expanding R & D in an effort to recover lost ground. We shall deal with this dilemma further at later points.

## FEDERAL GOVERNMENT R & D CONTRACTS

In an era in which the Federal Government of the United States finances some 60 percent of total private industry spending on R & D, Government R & D contracts are an obvious candidate for inclusion in our regression model. Certainly, in industries like aircraft and missiles and electric equipment, where the Government provides about 90 and 65 percent respectively of industry funds for R & D, the influence of Government finance would seem to be paramount. But even in industries where Government-sponsored R & D is a relatively small proportion of total R & D cost, Government finance can be influential, because many individual firms perform a great deal of Government contract work.

Probably the most important way in which Government R & D contracts can influence the scale of industry R & D activity is associated with the enhanced ability of the performing firms to acquire scientific and technical personnel. One obvious source of this ability is the increased size of R & D budgets that such work permits, including allowances for personnel that can be charged off to the Government. In addition, recruiting costs can be charged to overhead costs and are reimbursable in the case of contracts let by the Department of Defense (which accounts for some 75 percent of total Government R & D contracts). Also, with much Government R & D standing at the periphery of existing knowledge, the performing firms can often hold forth the promise of interesting and challenging work to prospective scientific personnel. Further, the discovery of new knowledge often enlarges the scientific base from which the performing firm operates and suggests new paths for research not directly connected with the Government contract; scientists working in industry have informed the writer that this is a quite common occurrence, and that scientific personnel are often moved off Government contract work to explore new ideas that have arisen in connection with this work.

Other influences are more subtle. Although apparently far short of the extent once hoped for, it remains true that some technological developments resulting from Government-financed R & D have direct and immediate commercial applications. But there are others whose commercial applicability is only in the potential stage at the completion of a Government contract; further developments and modifications are necessary before these are ready for the commercial market. However, the costs in this stage may be a relatively small part of the total R & D costs, and the fact that the bulk of the latter have already been paid for by the Government must certainly be viewed as an incentive to undertake the marginal developments and modifications needed for commercial markets.

In a number of cases, firms will bid for Government R & D contracts only when the R & D is relevant to technical—and hence commercial—problems already confronting them. The result is that although the firm may provide the Government with the sought-for product, the firm often acquires knowledge at Government expense that may be applied to its own problems and thereby reduce considerably the R & D costs of solving the latter.

The foregoing discussion implies a positive relation between a firm's R & D and Government R & D contracts. Although this would appear to be the most plausible relation, a negative one is also a possibility. Here and there one hears and reads remarks that an increase in Government-financed R & D necessitates a cutback in a firm's privately financed R & D. The reason usually given is limited scientific personnel, causing a reallocation from one set of projects to the other. This is not implausible. But it implies that for some reason, even though the total R & D budget is larger with the additional Federal funds, the firm either does not want to expand its R & D establishment despite its ability to afford to, or the additional Federal funds still do not enable it to afford to. The latter is consistent with a strong monopsonistic position of the firm in the market for scientific personnel, a realistic possibility in recent years in the United States, or it may imply other heavy marginal costs such as those stemming from additional facilities. The former may occur if the firm does not see any permanent future to expansion (that is, the Federal funds involve only a temporary increase in the total R & D budget) and doesn't want to upset morale at a later time by laying off scientific personnel. This decision may also imply that the firm does not envision any future growth in its own R & D, for if such growth is contemplated the added personnel could possibly be absorbed later on (unless it were very highly specialized).

In any case, it should not occasion much surprise if our statistical analysis turned up minus, as well as plus, signs for the coefficient of the Government R & D contract variable in our regression model.

### GROSS INVESTMENT IN PLANT AND EQUIPMENT

A significant proportion if not all of industry spending on R & D must be considered as a form of investment. This is true even though much of it is defensive in character, is but another way of achieving product differentiation, and is thus to a considerable extent featured by expectations of a payoff in less than five years.[6] For it is also true, according to numerous surveys, that much fixed investment by firms, particularly in machinery and equipment, is undertaken in the expectation of a similarly quick payoff. Accordingly, it is not unreasonable to view these two forms of investment as competitors for funds in any given current budget within which a firm decides to operate. This is not to deny the obvious and strong possibility that current R & D may act as a stimulus to *future* fixed investment in many results of the R & D, thereby implying a complementary relation between these variables. But such a possibility is fully consistent with a substitute relation between current R & D expenditures and *current* fixed-investment outlays, certainly within the context of some sort of a budget constraint.

Accordingly, we have included a variable for gross fixed investment in our regression, with the expectation of a minus sign for the coefficient of this variable. There is, however, one

[6] See p. 77.

source of doubt on this matter that can be mentioned. In 1954, the United States Internal Revenue Act was altered to permit firms to treat R & D as a current expense, and most firms have taken advantage of this change. In principle, such a change should not alter the substance of the aforementioned relation to fixed investment. But one cannot be sure, particularly since for budget purposes investment decisions are commonly made within the framework of a capital budget. At the same time, there is ample evidence that R & D expenditure *decisions* are *not* made in a manner comparable to those involving current costs; rather their treatment is very much analogous to the manner in which fixed-investment decisions are made. Still, the tax treatment does tend to obscure somewhat an otherwise clean-cut hypothesis.

PAST SCALE OF R & D

If the desirability of continuity and stability of research departments is as great as management often claims, then it follows that the current scale of R & D by the firm will be strongly influenced by past R & D. At the least, stability considerations may place an approximate (that is, somewhat elastic) floor beneath current scales of R & D. Beyond this, the well-known tendency of research to feed upon itself may cause past R & D to lead to future increases in this activity. Past R & D implies the existence not only of projects that must be continued to fruition but also the acquisition of new knowledge that often opens up vistas for new and expanded programs.

In our model the influence of the past on the present scale of R & D will be represented by lagged R & D. Our hypothesis will be that R & D tends to an important extent to be a continuing activity, but that adjustments will be made in accordance with sales or profits conditions and the other variables described above. As such, we have every reason to expect the coefficient of the lagged R & D variable to be positive in sign.

### Methods and Procedures

#### THE SAMPLE

Initially, a sample of 694 firms was collected. This group consisted, first, of 387 firms drawn from *Fortune* magazine's 500 industrials and used earlier in the study between size of firm and R & D. From this base the initial sample was built up to 694 from other sources, principally a list of recipients of R & D contracts from the Department of Defense. To get into this initial sample, a firm had to be listed in the 1960 edition of the National Research Council's *Industrial Research Laboratories of the United States*.[7] The reason was that the data on 1960 R & D by firm used in this study are R & D *personnel* as reported by company in this volume, data on R & D expenditures by firm not being published.

Unfortunately, the original sample of 694 firms had to be reduced in number, ultimately to 405. The reasons were many and varied. By far the most important, however, was unavailability of data on the independent variables of the foregoing model. With the exception of the data on R & D personnel and Government R & D contracts, almost all the data used in this study were taken from *Moody's Industrial Manual* for the years 1959 and 1960.[8] The rest were obtained from correspondence

---

[7] Baltimore, Waverly Press, 1960.

[8] New York, D. F. Shea, 1959 and 1960.

with over 100 companies.[9] But in many instances data were unavailable from either of these sources, and firms had to be dropped.

Mergers and related actions were another important reason for dropping firms. However, in the face of the spate of mergers of recent years, dropping all firms that were involved in mergers in 1959 and 1960 would have rendered most of our separate industry sample sizes too small for purposes of statistical analysis. At the same time, the principal reason for eliminating such firms is that mergers can induce large changes in property accounts without being immediately reflected in other accounts; but clearly the significance of this depends heavily on the size of the merger. For this reason, as well as to rescue our initial sample from possible annihilation, it was decided arbitrarily to drop only those firms whose property accounts changed by more than 20 percent.

The third major reason for dropping firms was that their closing dates for financial statements fell outside the interval September 30–March 31. Something of this sort obviously had to be done to gain a measure of consistency in the reporting and use of data. Firms with statements dated after January 1 were included with those of the previous year.

Fortunately, these reasons for omitting firms from the final sample often overlapped; otherwise, the reduction would have been considerably more drastic. However, we must also note that where subsidiaries were listed separately from parent companies in both *Moody's* and the directory of industrial laboratories, they have been treated separately in this study; other subsidiaries were combined with the parent companies.

When the final total of firms had been reached, the 405 firms

9 Because most of the information thus obtained was given on assurance of secrecy, it has not been possible to reveal the names of the firms included in the present study.

were then distributed over the twenty-one two- and three-digit industry groups listed below in Table 8. Each firm was classified in a single industry group on the basis of its major product.[10] In an R & D study by firm there is really little choice. The only other basis possible would have been with the establishment as the reporting unit; although much industry data is collected on this basis, R & D data are not and could not be, since R & D is definitely not an establishment activity.[11] But since many companies with large R & D programs have establishments classified in a variety of industries, we caution the reader that data reported in the following pages may not be compared directly with other industry data that have been compiled using the establishment as the basic unit.

All the industry groups listed in Table 8 are in the manufacturing sector. However, three companies normally classified in the communications industry were included in the manufacturing industry group described as "electronic components and communications equipment," [12] because of substantial similarities in many producing and R & D activities.

[10] Based on product-line information contained in *Poor's Register of Directors and Executives, 1960* (New York, Standard and Poor's Corp., 1960), which gives four-digit product classes for each company, and *Moody's Industrial Manual, 1960* (*loc. cit.*).

[11] See pp. 86-87.

[12] This industry group embraces the 1957 Standard Industrial Classification (SIC) categories, developed and employed by the Bureau of Census, 366-67; the three companies in question would normally be in SIC 48. For those interested, the industry groups listed in Table 8 below embrace the following SIC two- and three-digit numbers, starting at the top with Aircraft and missiles: 372, 281-82, 283, 284-89, 366-67, 361-69, except for 366-67, 34, 20, 352-53, 354-55, 357, balance of SIC 35, 26, 29, 331-32, 333-39, 38, 30, 32, 22, 37 except for 372.

## THE DATA

As indicated earlier, because of the absence of published data on R & D expenditures by firm, we have had to use total R & D personnel data by firm published by the National Research Council. These data are collected by means of a mailed questionnaire, which contains instructions about the kinds of work that are to be included under R & D. Nevertheless, the responding firms must, of course, make the final decision about whom to include and exclude, and this naturally raises questions—unanswerable—about the reliability of the data. Other sources of doubt on this score include some incentive to exaggerate the reported figures in an age that looks approvingly on firms apparently conducting much R & D; conversely, firms may, for competitive reasons, feel inclined to understate their figures, although this seems less likely, because they are under no legal obligation to respond at all to the questionnaire. Notwithstanding these doubts about their reliability, we have been constrained to use this source of data for want of any other source on a comparable scale.

We must note also that the National Research Council has been conducting its surveys in recent years only every five years. For the lagged R & D variable, therefore, the most recent figures available were those for 1955. In the face of the generally rapid growth in industrial R & D during the 1950's, these seemed much too far removed from 1960 to be used for the lagged variable. Therefore, to generate data for the year 1959 resort was made to the device of linear extrapolation between 1955 and 1960.

The data on sales used were net (after discounts and rebates) sales. As mentioned above, the data for this variable as well as those for profit, depreciation, and gross investment, were taken from *Moody's Industrial Manual* for the years 1959 and 1960. The profits variable chosen for this study was net (after-tax) profits (sometimes called net income to surplus). This particular concept of profits seems to be about as good a measure of a firm's profit expectations as can be obtained. Moreover, since net profits comprise a major proportion of cash flows, it also seems to serve well as a liquidity variable. For the other liquidity variable, depreciation, the data on current depreciation expense were used.

Lagged and unlagged values were tried for each of these variables. Simple zero-order correlations were run for each of the twenty-one industries between R & D for 1960 and each of the lagged and unlagged values of the three variables. The decision to use in the multiple-regression model a lagged or un-lagged variable in each case was made on the basis of the higher correlation coefficient.

The choice of data to represent gross investment was a difficult one. After much deliberation, the variable change in gross fixed assets for 1960 (that is, the difference between plant and equipment book values for 1959 and 1960) was chosen over the more conventional current purchases of fixed capital goods. As described earlier, a gross-investment variable was included in the model to represent a competing use of investment funds, on the grounds that much R & D is treated as a form of investment activity. Now the difference between the above two concepts of gross investment is largely equal to receipts from the sales of used capital goods. To the extent that expenditures of investment funds on new capital goods are offset by revenues from the sales of used ones, these gross expenditures overstate the use of the aggregate pool of investment funds. In other words, this pool should legitimately be defined to include funds derived from the sale of used assets, because these funds are truly available to finance further investment outlays in the same way as depreciation allowances, and in all probability are so used. Failure to use such funds for investment purposes would mean that the firm's capital is not being kept intact, in exactly the same way as would the use of depreciation allowances for other than gross investment.

Finally, data on Government R & D contracts were taken from lists of the 500 largest contractors put out by the Department of Defense (DOD) for the years 1955-1960 inclusive. DOD in 1960 accounted for approximately 75 percent of all Federal Government R & D contracts. Although lists from agencies other than DOD were available, the reported figures were not comparable and hence could not be combined with those of DOD.

Limitation of the DOD lists to the 500 largest contractors raised serious questions about the feasibility of using this data. But since no other data on Government R & D contracts by firm are available, the choice was either to drop this variable from our regression or make do as best as possible with the available data. Because of the apparent importance of Government contracts in a number of industries, it seemed better to pursue the latter tack—while hoisting warning signals for the reader.

Obviously, almost anything done along such lines would be quite arbitrary; so there seems little point in discussing more than the course actually taken. Briefly, then, three regressions were run of the entire model described earlier. The first, reported in Table 6 below, was based on DOD contracts let during the year 1960 only and was confined to those eight industries in which at least one third of the firms were on this list. The cutoff point on this list was contracts with a value of $140,000. Those firms in the eight industries not on this list were treated as having contracts of zero value. On the assumption that contracts of smaller magnitude would exert minimal influence on the scale of a firm's R & D activities, this does not appear to be particularly objectionable procedure.

For what it is worth, the writer's opinion is that the greatest confidence can be placed in the results for the aircraft and missiles, electronic components and communication equipment, and other electric equipment industries, where the proportion of firms having 1960 contracts was 95, 70, and 63 percent respectively. And although the industrial-chemicals industry just met the one-third criterion, a fair amount of confidence may be placed in the results of its regression, because other evidence indicates that relatively few firms perform R & D work for the Government, and those that do tend to be the fairly large ones that appear on the 1960 DOD list. About the others too little is known by the writer to render a judgment.

Based on 1960 DOD data alone, the eight regression results reported in Table 6 imply a lagless relation between R & D and these contracts, possibly a questionable relation, although defensible if contracts by firm are highly correlated over time, as they give some evidence of being. It is arguable that to the extent that a firm's R & D establishment is expanded in response to R & D contracts, for a number of reasons expansion is inevitably gradual, and considerable time may elapse before the buildup is completed.[13] Hence, it was decided to rerun the regressions using the sum of DOD contracts for each firm over the period 1955-60, inclusive, for three industries, and a similar sum for the period 1958-60, inclusive, for one industry. Because of the aforementioned coverage problems, it seemed sufficient to limit the first of the reruns to the aircraft and missiles, electronic components and communication equipment, and

---

[13] There is much truth in this statement, but it can easily be exaggerated. In many instances firms must do a large amount of preliminary research on their own before they can apply for a Government R & D contract.

other electric equipment industries, and the second rerun to the aircraft and missile industry alone. Not only was coverage best, by far, in these industries, but the vast bulk of Federal funds for R & D to industry—about 80 percent—goes to these three industry groups, 55 percent going to the aircraft and missile industry alone.[14] The results of these two reruns are reported in Table 7.

Aside from the eight industries shown in Table 6, most of the remaining industries had no more than one to five firms (in our final sample) with DOD contracts. For this reason, and because other industry data show that many of these industries receive quite small Government R & D contracts, it was decided to drop the Government contract variable and run the remainder of the model for these industries. At the same time, because the regressions that included this variable leave something to be desired, and also because it was felt desirable to see how the eight industries included in Table 6 compared with the other thirteen in the regressions without the Government contract variable, these eight were included in the latter regressions. The results for all twenty-one industries are set forth in Table 8.

### HETEROSCEDASTICITY AND SIZE-DEFLATED DATA

A basic assumption underlying the use of least-squares correlation and regression models like that employed in the present study is homoscedasticity, that is constant variance of the disturbance term with respect to the explanatory variables. With the use of cross-section data, however, such as those used in

---

[14] In each of the reruns for these industries, firms not appearing on the DOD list in any given year were coded as having zero contracts for that year. The cutoff figure in the contract lists falls increasingly below $140,000 as we proceed back from 1960, falling to $70,000 in 1955.

this study, this assumption is rarely met. Instead, substantial heteroscedasticity is usually present; that is, error variance tends to increase with the values of the independent variables. In studies like the present one, this is not difficult to understand. Large firms tend to have large sales, profits, depreciation allowances, Government R & D contracts, gross investments, *and* large R & D establishments; the opposite tends to be true of small firms. As a result, it is difficult to get an accurate picture of the relation between a firm's R & D and the explanatory variables of the model: the influence of size is always intruding.

To achieve as much homoscedasticity as possible, we followed what has become the fairly conventional procedure of deflating our data by means of size variables.[15] All but the R & D variables were deflated by gross fixed assets, lagged one year in each case. Other things equal, it would have been desirable to deflate the R & D variables with the same deflator(s), but since data for the former were R & D employment, it seemed more meaningful to use unlagged total employment as deflators for these.[16]

---

[15] The problems associated with and the use of size deflators to correct for heteroscedasticity are discussed at length in E. Kuh and J. R. Meyers, "Correlation and Regression Estimates When the Data Are Ratios," *Econometrica*, 23 (October 1955), pp. 400-416.

[16] Examination of the raw data indicated that they tended to satisfy rather well the condition of linear homogeneity between the deflator variables and the remaining ones. As Kuh and Meyer have shown (*loc. cit.*), this condition is sufficient to assure that a multiple correlation between deflated ratio variables will yield an unbiased estimate of the relation between the numerator series with the influence of the deflator variables held constant.

Logarithmic transformation of the raw data is another common method for eliminating heteroscedasticity. But it is a monotonic transformation, leaving the correction incomplete. Furthermore, a linear least-squares regression on logarithmic data implies a multiplicative relation among the explanatory variables in the original hypothesis. Such a relation implies, in turn, that the effect of any one of these variables upon the dependent variable depends on the values of the other variables. Some such relation may exist between the depreciation and sales (profits) variables, but there seems to be no basis

The use of deflated data has another advantage for this study. Cross-section data based on business firms tends to pose the real danger that extreme values associated with large firms will lead to false product-moment computations, thus giving rise to spurious correlation and regression coefficients. By eliminating the influence of size, deflation helps to assure that extreme values will have a negligible effect on parameter estimates.

The use of ratio variables also has the advantage of enabling us to test for the influences upon R & D intensity, in this case R & D employment as a proportion of total employment. Little is known about what factors determine differences in R & D intensity.[17] The results of the present study, because they are based on ratio variables, can be used for this purpose. And this is true even though our hypotheses pertain to undeflated variables; for reasons stated in footnote 16, our results can be used to test our hypotheses in this form. But this does not prevent us from also utilizing them to test for influences upon R & D intensity.

### The Basic R & D Models

In line with the hypotheses and procedures described above, the following models were specified for multiple, least-squares regression. For the eight industries shown in Table 6,

$$\frac{R_{1960}}{E_{1960}} = f\left( \frac{P_{1960}}{K_{1959}} \text{ or } \frac{P_{1959}}{K_{1958}}, \frac{D_{1960}}{K_{1959}} \text{ or } \frac{D_{1959}}{K_{1958}}, \frac{G_{1960}}{K_{1959}}, \frac{I_{1960}}{K_{1959}}, \frac{R_{1959}}{E_{1959}}, u \right)$$

---

for the same to be true among all the others. For this and other reasons, the alternative of a logarithmic transformation of the data was rejected.

[17] Apropos of an earlier remark (p. 116), one ostensible influence on R & D intensity, *viz.*, size of firm, has been shown to be virtually nonexistent. See pp. 58-63.

$$\frac{R_{1960}}{E_{1960}} = g\left(\frac{S_{1960}}{K_{1959}}, \frac{D_{1960}}{K_{1959}} \text{ or } \frac{D_{1959}}{K_{1958}}, \frac{G_{1960}}{K_{1959}}, \frac{I_{1960}}{K_{1959}}, \frac{R_{1959}}{E_{1959}}, u\right),$$

where $R$ is R & D personnel, $P$ is after-tax profits, $S$ is net sales, $D$ is current depreciation expense, $G$ is Government (DOD) R & D contracts, $I$ is gross investment (as defined earlier), $E$ is total employment, $K$ is gross fixed assets, and $u$ is a stochastic disturbance term. It should be obvious that the above two equations are identical except for the interchange of profits and sales. To include both variables in the regression would introduce a serious problem of multicollinearity and hence a problem of indeterminacy. Note that the inclusion of depreciation charges in those regressions containing the sales, but not the profits, variable permits us to test separately for some of the influence of internal sources of finance on R & D.

For the three industries shown in the top part of Table 7, the same regressions were fitted, except that in place of the deflated 1960 Government contracts variable, the variable used was the *sum* of DOD contracts for each firm over the period 1955-60, inclusive, with this variable also deflated by $K_{1959}$. The coefficients shown for the aircraft and missile industry in the lower half of Table 7 were also obtained from the same regressions, except that in this case the Government contracts variable used was the sum of DOD contracts for each firm over the period 1958-60, again deflated by $K_{1959}$.

With the exception of the Government contracts variable, which was dropped altogether, the same regressions were run for the twenty-one industries shown in Table 8.

## Empirical Results

### THE GOVERNMENT CONTRACT MODELS

We may begin our examination of the statistical results with the model, for eight industries, containing the Government contract variable. We shall concentrate the discussion on this variable at this point, being quite terse in dealing with the others. The reason is that, as between this model and the one that excludes this variable, for the overlapping eight industries the sign of only one of the coefficients of the remaining variables changes, and this coefficient is not statistically significant in either model. Hence there seems little point in trodding the same path twice.

Looking at Table 6, we observe from the *"t"* values given in parentheses that, taking the profits and sales variables together, there are five out of eight coefficients with minus signs, of which three are statistically significant; of the remaining three with plus signs, one is significant.[18] Six out of eight coefficients of depreciation have a minus sign, one of which is significant, while the remaining two have a plus sign, of which, again, one is significant. Skipping the Government contract variable for the moment, we can also see that five out of the eight coefficients of the gross-investment variable have minus signs, and three of these are significant; of the three with plus signs, none is significant. Not surprisingly, all eight coefficients of the R & D variable have plus signs, and seven of the eight are significant.[19]

---

[18] The *"t"* values given in parentheses are the quotients obtained, in conventional fashion, by dividing the partial regression coefficients by their respective standard errors.

**Table 6** *Partial Regression Coefficients for Government Contract Model, Eight Manufacturing Industries, 1960*

| Industry | Sample Size | Profits | Sales | Depreciation | Government Contracts | Gross Investment | R & D Personnel, 1959 | $R^2$ | F |
|---|---|---|---|---|---|---|---|---|---|
| Aircraft and missiles | 20 | — | -0.311* (-2.200) | -0.015† (-0.351) | 0.001 (0.150) | -0.203* (-2.398) | 1.166** (8.226) | .87 | 19.3** |
| Industrial chemicals | 34 | -0.168** (-3.004) | — | 0.453** (2.820) | 1.245** (5.220) | -0.367** (-2.900) | 1.206** (17.148) | .96 | 142.6** |
| Electronic components and communications equipment | 24 | -0.285†** (-3.033) | — | -1.509†* (-2.640) | 0.170** (3.258) | -0.013 (-1.900) | 0.531** (3.070) | .79 | 14.1** |
| Other electrical equipment | 27 | -0.112 (-1.550) | — | -0.006† (-0.176) | 0.177** (2.567) | 0.025 (1.450) | 0.999** (16.999) | .97 | 127.2** |
| Office machines | 12 | — | 0.051** (4.776) | 0.023 (1944) | 0.073** (10.729) | -0.364 (-1.760) | 0.894** (44.599) | .99 | 105.9** |
| Professional and scientific instruments | 18 | -0.069 (-0.600) | — | -0.573 (-0.694) | 0.037 (0.232) | 0.142 (1.102) | 0.788* (2.232) | .49 | 2.3 |
| Rubber products | 16 | 0.111† (0.779) | — | -0.490† (-0.813) | -0.057 (-0.172) | 0.033 (0.760) | 0.448 (2.093) | .38 | 1.4 |
| Other transportation equipment | 18 | — | 0.010 (0.650) | -0.218 (-1.825) | -0.157 (-0.969) | -0.426* (-2.271) | 1.079** (8.907) | .95 | 47.9** |

† 1959 value    * significant at .05 level    ** significant at .01 level

**Table 7** Partial Regression Coefficients for Government Contract Model Using $\sum_{1955}^{1960}$ Contracts for Three Manufacturing Industries, and $\sum_{1958}^{1960}$ Contracts for One, 1960

| Industry | Sample Size | Profits | Sales | Depreciation | Government Contracts | Gross Investment | R & D Personnel, 1959 | $R^2$ | F |
|---|---|---|---|---|---|---|---|---|---|
| Aircraft and missiles | 20 | — | -0.311* (-2.399) | -0.042† (-0.897) | 0.004 (1.000) | -0.203* (-2.416) | 1.112** (8.613) | .88 | 20.8** |
| Electronic components and communications equipment | 24 | 0.019† (0.160) | — | 0.215† (0.289) | 0.007 (0.506) | -0.001 (-1.013) | 0.540** (3.650) | .48 | 3.4* |
| Other electrical equipment | 27 | -0.106 (-0.251) | — | -0.089†** (-3.004) | -0.091* (-2.086) | 0.023 (1.349) | 1.005** (18.091) | .97 | 127.1** |
| Aircraft and missiles | 20 | — | -0.311 (-2.028) | -0.011† (-0.307) | 0.002 (0.387) | -0.202* (-2.279) | 1.133** (7.850) | .87 | 19.5** |

† 1959 value    * significant at .05 level    ** significant at .01 level

Turning now to the variable of chief interest in this model, the Government contract variable, we find that six of the eight coefficients have a plus sign, and four of these six are significant; of the two that have minus signs, neither is significant. Even though we earlier raised the possibility that presumably statistically significant minus signs might arise, these results probably occasion little surprise. What is surprising is the failure of this coefficient to turn out to be significantly greater than zero in the aircraft and missile industry, where some 90 percent of R & D expenditures have been financed from Government contracts. For reasons discussed earlier, it was at first thought that this result was the product of a poor choice for this variable and that if Government contracts were summed over a (varying) period of years, to allow for gradualness in the response to such contracts, a significant result would follow. But as can be seen in Table 7, neither a five- nor two-year sum of such contracts has any effect on the coefficient of this variable in the aircraft and missile industry.[20]

Furthermore, for all the industries shown in the upper part of Table 7, it is noteworthy that the zero-order simple correlations appearing in the correlation matrix conform with the results obtained in multiple-correlation analyses. Thus, with the 1960 data for the Government contracts variable, the zero-order correlation coefficient for the aircraft and missile indus-

---

[19] Although we have included in all the tables the multiple coefficients of determination, $R^2$, and their F ratios, too much stress should not be placed upon them, even though most of them indicate "goodness of fit" for each industry that is quite high. The reason is that, given the great stability of R & D activity in most industries, any R & D model that includes lagged R & D among the explanatory variables will tend to yield a high $R^2$.

[20] In fact, using the five-year sum, although producing no significant changes in the results for the entire model in the cases of the aircraft and missile and other electric equipment industries, does produce significant changes in the electronics industry—all for the worse. Besides the change in sign of the

try ($= .32$) is not significant at the .05 level, whereas in the electronics and other electric equipment industries this same coefficient ($= .56$ and .62, respectively) is significant at the .01 level, thus paralleling closely the significance levels of the regression coefficients of this variable for these two industries in Table 6. In a similar manner, of the coefficients for the Government contract variable shown in Table 7, only that for the other electric equipment industry is significant, and the same is true of the zero-order correlation coefficient in this case.

Thus, for reasons that defy explanation by one person, it appears that in one of the industries in which a priori expectations suggested that its influence on R & D would be strongest, the Government contract variable turns out to be of no apparent significance, statistically and otherwise.

THE MODEL EXCLUDING THE GOVERNMENT
CONTRACT VARIABLE

Given the vagaries in the Government contract data, there is room for considerably more confidence in the results of this model and, since it has been run for all twenty-one of our industry groups, for more interest as well. Because profits may function either as a finance variable, with plus sign, or as an indicator of future profits, with plus *or* minus sign, we might well begin our discussion of the results of this model by examining the coefficients of the liquidity variable per se, namely, depreciation, for evidence on the importance of a firm's liquidity as an influence on R & D. Although the reader may find

coefficient of the profits variable, note that this variable as well as that for Government contracts becomes statistically nonsignificant and that the value of $R^2$ drops sharply.

**Table 8** Partial Regression Coefficients for Twenty-One Manufacturing Industries, 1960
(Model Excluding Government Contract Variable)

| Industry | Sample Size | Profits | Sales | Depreciation | Gross Investment | R & D Personnel, 1959 | $R^2$ | F |
|---|---|---|---|---|---|---|---|---|
| Aircraft and missiles | 20 | — | −0.498* (−2.187) | −0.012† (−0.332) | −0.282* (−2.156) | 1.162** (9.776) | .87 | 25.8** |
| Industrial chemicals | 34 | −0.258** (−3.507) | — | 0.784** (3.847) | −0.493** (−3.022) | 1.396** (16.800) | .92 | 89.9** |
| Drugs and medicines | 19 | 0.339†* (2.913) | — | −0.123† (−2.071) | −0.239* (−2.267) | 0.959** (27.766) | .98 | 338.8** |
| Other chemicals | 16 | — | 0.325* (2.315) | −0.227† (−2.048) | −0.302* (−2.263) | 1.070†* (4.444) | .99 | 542.6** |
| Electronic components and communications equipment | 24 | −0.344†** (−3.827) | — | −1.400†* (−2.145) | −0.047* (−2.505) | 0.553** (3.153) | .73 | 11.1** |
| Other electrical equipment | 27 | −0.349** (−2.985) | −0.041 (−0.707) | −0.051† (−2.040) | 0.094 (0.564) | 0.964** (17.103) | .91 | 137.2** |
| Fabricated metals | 17 | — | — | 0.002† (0.947) | −0.044 (−1.954) | 1.049** (55.512) | .96 | 731.0** |
| Food and kindred products | 22 | −0.132† (−1.875) | — | 0.070 (1.274) | −0.348* (−2.717) | 1.112 (45.552) | .99 | 533.5** |
| Extractive, construction, and conveyance equipment | 16 | — | 0.024 (1.424) | 0.153† (1.429) | −0.227** (−4.296) | 1.397** (48.464) | .97 | 738.7** |

| Industry | | A | B | C | D | E | $R^2$ | F |
|---|---|---|---|---|---|---|---|---|
| Machine tools and special industry machinery | 17 | — | 0.068 (0.138) | 0.425+* (2.623) | −0.187* (−2.316) | 1.151** (6.486) | .81 | 13.1** |
| Office machines | 12 | — | 0.279** (9.193) | −0.014 (−0.298) | −0.362* (−2.513) | 1.097** (31.495) | .95 | 755.4** |
| Other machinery | 15 | −0.047+ (−0.549) | — | 0.022 (0.306) | 0.051 (0.409) | 0.961** (19.013) | .97 | 103.2** |
| Paper and allied products | 29 | 0.424+** (2.742) | — | −0.024 (−0.567) | 0.002 (0.025) | 0.840** (24.849) | .96 | 163.9** |
| Petroleum and petroleum products | 16 | −0.102* (−2.286) | — | −0.048+ (−1.604) | 0.059 (2.157) | 1.079** (33.834) | .96 | 326.4** |
| Primary ferrous products | 20 | — | 0.244** (3.738) | 0.032+ (0.291) | −0.277* (−2.899) | 0.171 (0.442) | .65 | 6.8** |
| Primary nonferrous products | 18 | 0.587* (2.405) | — | 0.168 (0.562) | −0.411** (−4.421) | 0.373* (2.495) | .82 | 15.0** |
| Professional and scientific instruments | 18 | −0.070 (−0.629) | — | −0.475 (−0.695) | 0.138 (1.121) | 0.822* (2.788) | .49 | 3.1 |
| Rubber products | 16 | 0.106+ (0.796) | — | −0.539+ (−1.059) | 0.034 (0.859) | 0.448 (2.191) | .37 | 1.7 |
| Stone, clay, and glass products | 17 | 0.007+ (0.181) | — | −0.279 (−1.854) | 0.046* (2.563) | 0.942** (6.022) | .91 | 32.0** |
| Textiles | 13 | −0.252* (−3.229) | — | 0.063* (2.465) | 0.001 (0.128) | 0.791** (14.854) | .92 | 68.3** |
| Other transportation equipment | 18 | — | 0.011 (0.809) | −0.171 (−1.572) | −0.524* (−2.206) | 1.105** (9.398) | .92 | 59.9** |

+ 1959 value     * significant at .05 level     ** significant at .01 level

room for disagreement, in the writer's judgment the results in Table 8 indicate rather little influence exerted by liquidity. First of all, only four of the twenty-one coefficients of the depreciation variable are significant. Secondly, twelve are marked by minus—the wrong—signs, and nine by plus signs. It is true that three of the four significant coefficients have plus signs, but in two industries (industrial chemicals and textiles) where this is so they are accompanied by significantly *negative* profits coefficients, which is the wrong sign from a liquidity standpoint. One would suppose that if the liquidity influence were strong in a given industry, it would show up significantly in both the profits and depreciation variables, or at least in a noncontradictory manner in the profits variable. Further, in three industries (drugs, other chemicals, and other electrical equipment) where the coefficients have minus signs but are not significant, they just miss being so, and in the stone, clay, and glass products industry, the negative coefficient is significant at .10.[21]

If the reader accepts the foregoing judgment about the influence of liquidity on R & D, then he will concur, too, in the correlative judgment that profits function not as a liquidity variable but along with sales as a gauge of future profitability. Therefore, looking at the coefficients of the profits and sales variable together, we find that there are eleven with plus signs and ten with minus signs. This same margin of difference holds up when we limit our attention to the eleven statistically significant coefficients, six of which have plus signs and five of which have minus signs. We remind the reader that there are

[21] Concentrating on those eight industries containing the sales but not the profits variable—to test separately for the influence of depreciation—does not provide much basis for altering our conviction regarding the weakness of the liquidity influence. There are four minus and four plus signs for the coefficient of the depreciation variable in these cases; two of the positive coefficients are significant, and one of the negative ones just misses at .05.

good and plausible a priori reasons for expecting the signs of these coefficients to go either way—plus or minus, and apparently there is nothing in our results to enable us to say which is the dominant reaction of R & D to changes in current sales and profits.

Leaving it to the reader to speculate further on this matter, we turn our attention to the gross-investment coefficients. Here we may say, with some confidence, that if there is any influence of this variable on R & D activities by the firm, it is the one hypothesized earlier. Thus, although only (?) thirteen of the twenty-one gross-investment coefficients have the expected minus sign, twelve of these are significant, whereas only one of the eight with the theoretically wrong sign is significant. Given the degree of diversity of behavior one would expect among different industries,[22] it may be somewhat unreasonable to look for stronger confirmation of a given hypothesis.

Having said this, we find, upon examination of the results of the lagged R & D variable, that all twenty-one coefficients have the hypothesized plus sign, and nineteen of these are significant. But as remarked earlier, in the face of the pressures to maintain continuity in any serious R & D program, it would have been little short of astonishing were these results otherwise.

---

[22] Note, however, the tendency toward similar patterns of behavior of all coefficients among three-digit industry groups that belong to the same two-digit industries.

# 7 Evaluation and Choice of Industrial Research and Development Projects: The Method of Linear Programming

The problem of evaluating and choosing among potential R & D projects in industry has been the subject of much discussion in the literature on R & D. Various formulae have been projected, and most, if not all, of them are apparently used by different companies.[1] These formulae seem to have been developed by management people anxious to rescue R & D project evaluation and choice from the morass into which it has evidently fallen. This is surely a worthy objective, but unfortunately the proposed formulae, which are used, are uniformly deficient in economic content. Although not all formulae are

---

[1] Discussions of these formulae may be found in F. Olsen, "The Control of Research Funds," in A. H. Rubinstein, ed., *Coordination, Control, and Financing of Industrial Research* (New York, Columbia University Press, 1955), p. 99; R. H. Manley, "Translating the Economic Aspects of Company Policy into Research Policy," *ibid.*, p. 160; T. T. Miller, "Projecting the Profitability of New Projects," *The Commercialization of Research Results*, Special Report No. 20 (New York, American Management Association, 1957), p. 31; W. C. Asbury, "Establishing Research Projects," in *Handbook of Industrial Research Management*, C. Heyel, ed. (New York, Reinhold Publishing Corporation, 1959), p. 201; J. B. Quinn, "Budgeting For Research," *ibid.*, p. 298; B. H. Rosen and A. L. Regnier, "Economics and Research Programming," *Chemical and Engineering Progress*, 52 (December 1956), 500-502.

equally guilty of the same lapses, as a group they are variously deficient in the following major respects:

(1) Failure to use probability distributions, instead of point estimates, in estimating costs and receipts associated with R & D projects as well as the technical feasibility of these projects. Precise estimates will usually not be feasible because of uncertainty about future events, but the choice among alternatives can be improved by considering the best available approximations. Thus, the more uncertain is the future, the greater will be the statistical variance around a probability estimate of the most likely events. Ignoring this variance means omission of useful information from the decision-making process. Yet even those formulae that do make use of probability estimates in R & D project evaluations omit consideration of the variances of these estimates.

(2) Complete neglect of the time pattern of receipts and costs. By failing to capitalize discount revenues and expenditures of different time periods with an appropriate rate of interest, the formulae treat these items as being of equal value, contrary to fact. This omission leads at once to incorrect measures of economic worth of R & D projects and a failure to consider alternative uses of capital funds.

(3) Use of the unnecessarily crude concept of the pay-out period (the length of time needed to recover an initial investment) as a way of handling the time distribution of revenues and expenditures. This method emphasizes liquidity and the turnover of capital to the exclusion of all other economic considerations.

(4) Use of various rates-of-return measures for ranking R & D projects as though these projects were unrelated to one another. But R & D projects are always interrelated, if for no other reason than the fact that they are all competing for scarce funds. Yet perusal of the literature on evaluation and choice

of R & D projects discloses the uniform omission of a budget constraint. Every R & D program, however, is faced with limited funds—that is, a budget constraint, not only in the present, but over time. In such circumstances, it is simply impossible to develop any economically meaningful project-evaluation formula without explicitly taking this constraint into account. In particular, it is not possible to *rank* projects accurately on the basis of rates of return or any other criteria without considering, *in the process of developing their ranks,* their interrelationships through the budget constraints.

The application of a method of deriving an optimum *set* of R & D projects is the subject of this chapter. The method is that of linear programming. This technique has been successfully employed in dealing with so many other business and economic problems of a comparable nature that it is surprising, indeed, that management has not seen fit to make use of it in evaluating and choosing R & D projects. As a technique applied to this problem, linear programming requires much the same sorts of estimates found in existing formulae. Thus, for example, costs and revenues must still be estimated, and on a probability basis; these streams must still be discounted to the present, and this means that an appropriate rate of discount must be decided upon in advance; and, finally, management must still determine how much funds are to be allocated to the company's R & D program over the planning period for which the budget is fixed—and these budgets, too, must be discounted to the present to ascertain their present values. Hence, it is not in these areas that linear programming offers any advantages vis-à-vis presently used formulae. Rather, it is in the choice of the optimal set of R & D projects from among the larger set that management is confronted with at the beginning of the planning period that linear programming has much to offer.

In setting forth the manner in which this technique may be thus applied, some familiarity on the part of the reader with linear programming must necessarily be assumed. The reader's indulgence is requested, since this is clearly no place to embark on an exposition of the fundamentals of this technique. At the same time there is a host of introductory texts on this subject, many of which demand no more from the reader than a knowledge of algebra. In any event, it behooves anyone involved in R & D project evaluations to become familiar with this method, because it represents the only escape known to the writer from poor jobs performed by even the more sophisticated of the above-mentioned formulae.

### The R & D Linear-Programming Model

Let us take our goal, a standard one, to be the selection of R & D projects that will maximize the present worth of the firm. In this case, we desire a method or formula that will enable the firm to choose from among the set or group of candidate projects that subset whose aggregate present value is greater than that of any other subset, subject to the condition that aggregate expenditures on this subset in any period of time be no greater than that permitted by the budget constraint of that period. The linear programming format applied to this twofold objective may be set forth as follows:

Maximize
$$\sum_{j=1}^{n} c_j x_j \tag{1}$$

Subject to
$$\sum_{j=1}^{n} a_{tj} x_j \leqslant B_t, \qquad t = 1, \ldots, T \tag{2}$$

$$0 \leqslant x_j \leqslant 1 \qquad j = 1, \ldots, n \qquad (3)$$

In this primal model, $c_j$ represents the net present value of R & D project $j$; by net present value is meant the discounted value of the stream of revenues accruing from the result of this project over its entire anticipated lifetime *minus* the discounted value of all the costs incurred in connection with both the R & D and the actual production and marketing of the result over its expected life.[2] $x_j$ is the symbol for each project $j$; in other words, $x_j$ $(j = 1, \ldots, n)$ is the set of projects in question, from which the aforementioned optimal subset must be chosen. $a_{tj}$ denotes the present discounted value of actual expenditures on project $j$ in each period $t$. $B_t$ is the present or discounted value of the amount of funds available for expenditure on all the potential projects in each period $t$; that is to say, $B_t$ is the budget constraint that is expected to prevail in each period $t$. In both instances, $t = 1, \ldots, T$, where $T$ represents the last period of the firm's planning time span (or horizon) in which outlays must be incurred and a budget constraint exists.

One feature of the above linear programming model deserves special mention. In addition to the non-negativity con-

[2] If the result of the R & D project is simply a cost-saving process, then in place of the stream of revenues must be substituted the discounted value of the stream of savings. In the case of new products, care must be taken to subtract from each period's revenues the loss of sales from items that are displaced by the new product.

In this analysis, we abstract from uncertainty, both in the interests of simplicity and focus; the need for probability estimates of revenues and costs, etc., has already been recognized in some project-evaluation formulae; but the usefulness of linear programming has not. Methods for incorporating uncertainty into linear programming may be found in W. W. Garvin, *Introduction to Linear Programming* (New York, McGraw-Hill, 1960), Ch. 12, and the references cited therein, p. 173.

Similarly, we avoid the problem of the appropriate rate of discount to be employed in capitalizing streams of revenues and costs. Presumably, it should be some market rate of interest, but which one is an involved question, and because it is, this is not the place to deal with it.

ditions imposed on the $x_j$ (which is characteristic of all such models), because a negative R & D project is palpable nonsense, we have imposed an upper bound of 1 on the $x_j$. This additional constraint is imposed to ensure that no more than one of any R & D project will appear in the optimal solution, the optimal subset of $x_j$, to the linear programming problem. Otherwise, $x_j$ would be free to take on any value $\geqslant 0$, implying the possibility of a large number of clearly undesirable, duplicate projects. At the same time, the upper bound of unity may appear to deprive the firm of the ability to experiment along different lines—that is, to conduct more than one R & D project—with the same goal in mind, a research approach that often pays dividends, especially when there are large gaps in basic knowledge in the area in question.[3] This is not so, however; duplicative R & D projects in this sense can be represented by the same $c_j$ in expression (1), with the different routes to the same goal expressed in the form of the different $a_{tj}$.[4]

We may also observe that the lower bounds shown in (3) permit the appearance of fractional R & D projects in the optimal subset. This possibility can be realistically interpreted as allowing some research projects to proceed at less than full tilt. Certainly, this approach goes on all the time in most industrial laboratories, in which some projects are given the full go-ahead, while others are either denied a full complement of research workers or are restricted in the amount of working time devoted to them. So there is no reason for keeping this possibility out of the optimal solution.

[3] See R. R. Nelson, "The Economics of Invention: A Survey of the Literature," *The Journal of Business*, 32 (April 1959), 113-114.

[4] The simpler, alternative approach of having desirably duplicative R & D projects appear in the form of allowing the $x_j$ to assume any value $\geqslant 0$ is not feasible, because the corresponding $a_{tj}$ would imply identical projects. A routine for solving linear programs with upper as well as lower bounds is described in Garvin, *op. cit.*, Ch. 11, and in references given there, p. 154.

Finally, and for later reference, we may note explicitly the meaning in the present context of the so-called slack variables, $s_t$, which must be added to expression (2) in order to convert these inequalities to equalities, preparatory to solving for the optimal subset of $x_j$. The $s_t$ may be interpreted as the discounted values of the unspent amounts of the budget constraints, $B_t$, in each period $t$. Since negative budget constraints are meaningless, the $s_t$ must also be constrained to be non-negative.

In addition, because of the upper bounds imposed on the $x_j$ in expression (3), it is necessary to add to (3) another set of slack variables, $y_j$, likewise constrained to non-negativity, to transform the inequalities $x_j \leqslant 1$ into equalities, also in preparation for obtaining the optimal subset of $x_j$. Since the modified (3) will then read $x_j + y_j = 1$, it is clear that the $y_j$ can attain values only between zero and one, inclusive, like the $x_j$. Thus, in the final, optimal solution to the above programming problem, a zero value for any particular $y_j$ implies a value of unity for the corresponding R & D project $x_j$; that is, a $y_j = 0$ means that the corresponding $x_j$ is included in its entirety in the optimal set of R & D projects. Contrariwise, a $y_j = 1$ means that the corresponding $x_j = 0$—that is, is excluded entirely from the optimal set of projects. And of course, a fractional value for any $y_j$ means a fractional value for the corresponding R & D project $x_j$ in the optimal set.

In some contrast, the $s_t$ in the optimal solution can assume any value from zero up to the corresponding budget constraint, $B_t$. A zero value for $s_t$ means the budget for that period $t$ is fully utilized; a positive value means that the latter is only partly utilized.

Beyond this, we cannot go into the details of the solution to the foregoing linear programming problem, except perhaps to say that it can be solved by a number of computational routines, the most commonly used being the so-called simplex method.[5] Whatever routine is used, however, by virtue of the program shown in (1)–(3), the set of projects selected will be the best—in the sense of maximizing the present value that can be derived from spending those sums that fall within the budget constraints, $B_t$. Further, it should be emphasized that the optimal subset of $x_j$, the one whose aggregate present value is greatest, will be obtained by the linear programming technique in the course of examining *all* the possible subsets of $x_j$ —subject, of course, to the conditions given in (2) and (3)— instead of one project at a time, as other R & D project-evaluation formulae incorrectly do. The significance of this fundamental difference will become apparent later on.

### The Dual Problem: Budget Costs and Project-Ranking Criteria

Every primal linear programming problem, like that above, has a so-called dual, and particularly in the analysis of economic problems the dual program often feeds out information of great importance. In the problem of evaluating and ranking R & D projects, this turns out to be especially true. Accordingly, the format for the dual of the foregoing primal, linear program may be presented immediately as follows:

Minimize
$$\sum_{t=1}^{T} \lambda_t B_t + \sum_{j=1}^{n} \delta_j \tag{4}$$

[5] An excellent discussion of this method, requiring no more than a knowledge of elementary algebra, is in Garvin, *op. cit.*, Ch. 2, p. 26 of which gives references to other computational routines such as the method of fictitious play and the complete-description method. Perhaps the most comprehensive discussion of linear programming, but one that requires some knowledge of matrix algebra, contained therein, is that of A. Charnes and W. W. Cooper, *Management Models and Industrial Applications of Linear Programming*, Vols. I and II (New York, John Wiley & Sons, 1961).

Subject to

$$\sum_{t=1}^{T} \lambda_t a_{tj} + \delta_j \geqslant c_j \tag{5}$$

$$\lambda_t, \delta_j \geqslant 0, \qquad t = 1, \ldots, T \tag{6}$$
$$j = 1, \ldots, n$$

As usual, this dual has as its objective the minimization of the total accounting costs to the firm of the scarce resources, in this case the budget constraints, $B_t$, and (in a manner to be discussed) the upper bounds imposed on the $x_j$ in (3). The $\lambda_t$ and the $\delta_j$ are two sets of so-called implicit, or accounting, or shadow prices or values. They are the unknowns to be solved by the dual program. So without further ado, let us examine the meaning of each of these sets of prices in the present context.

The $\lambda_t$, first of all, are implicit values of the budget constraints, $B_t$, in each period $t = 1, \ldots, T$. In the optimal solution of the dual program, they measure the present value of the increase in the dollar return per period associated with a $1 increment in each period's R & D budget. Thus, in a very real sense, the $\lambda_t$ are indicators to management of what it would be worth to alter the size of any particular period's budget, $B_t$. To an alert management this information must be every bit as important as the optimal subset of R & D projects derived from the primal program. Of course, if, as is likely, the size of the budget constraint differs among the successive periods $t = 1, \ldots, T$, and similarly the values of the $a_{tj}$, the values of the $\lambda_t$ will likewise vary. In fact, any particular $\lambda_t > 0$ only if the corresponding budget is used to the fullest; failing the fulfillment of the latter condition, $\lambda_t = 0$. This follows a basic dual-programming theorem that says, in effect, that the optimal accounting or shadow prices of an incompletely used resource must be zero. But this accords with economic intuition as well. For a resource that is not fully utilized is, in a reasonable sense, a free good.

The meaning of the $\delta_j$ is a bit more subtle, although, like the $\lambda_t$, they, too, are an implicit set of shadow prices. As the $\lambda_t$ are the implicit prices or costs of the budget constraints in the primal problem, so the $\delta_j$ are the implicit prices or costs, so to speak, of the $j = 1, \ldots, n$ conditions $x_j \leqslant 1$ of the same primal problem. Moreover, the $\delta_j$ set of implicit prices of this dual obey the same rules as any other more conventional dual price variable. That is to say, they are positive when in the optimal solution the fixed resource is used to the limit, and zero when the fixed resource is less than fully utilized. Thus the $\delta_j > 0$ when the corresponding R & D project $x_j$ that appears in the optimal solution equals 1; and $\delta_j = 0$ if the corresponding $x_j$ of the optimal subset is less than 1.[6] Hence the $\delta_j$ can be viewed as *evaluators of accepted R & D projects* in the optimal solution to the earlier primal problem.

Continuing to apply conventional duality theorems, we may give more concrete economic content to the $\delta_j$ as the set of implicit evaluators of accepted projects by noting that for any $x_j$ ($> 0$) in the optimal subset, the corresponding dual inequality in expression (5) must become an equality; this is an extension of the basic duality condition that the implicit (unit) costs of any $x_j$ that appears in the optimal solution must equal the unit profits associated with that $x_j$. Viewing (5), then, as an equality in the optimal solution, and transposing

$\sum\limits_{t=1}^{T} \lambda_t a_{tj}$ to the right-hand side of (5), we may interpret $\delta_j$ as

$c_j - \sum\limits_{t=1}^{T} \lambda_t a_{tj}$; in other words, $\delta_j$ is the net present value of

---

[6] Of course, $\delta_j = 0$ for any particular $x_j$ that is excluded entirely from the optimal set of R & D projects.

accepted project $x_j$ minus the present value of all future expenditures on $x_j$ valued in each period at the implicit price, $\lambda_t$, of the budget constraint.[7] Further, since the $\delta_j$ will in general have different values for those accepted $x_j = 1$, they provide management with a basis for *ranking* these projects.

But we must remember that $\delta_j = c_j - \sum_{t=1}^{T} \lambda_j a_{tj} > 0$, only if

the corresponding $x_j = 1$ in the optimal solution of the primal problem. For any such $0 < x_j < 1$, that is, for a fractional project in the optimal subset, $\delta_j = 0$, as noted earlier. Of what use can these $\delta_j$ be in a ranking of accepted projects? The answer is that for these fractional projects for which $\delta_j = 0$, the firm is on the margin of indifference—completely so. So far as the maximum present value of the optimal subset of $x_j$, including the fractional projects, is concerned, the latter do not

---

[7] For those readers familiar with the more common lower-bound conditions of non-negativity alone on the $x_j$, we may call attention to the contrast between the above result and the more common one, without upper bounds, in which

$$c_j - \sum_{t=1}^{T} \lambda_t a_{tj} = 0$$ as the condition for acceptance of any $x_j$ in the optimal

solution of a linear program. The latter condition implies, of course, that the imputed prices of the scarce factors, in the present case the $\lambda_t$, are always high enough in the optimal solution of the dual (*sans* upper bounds) to render profits to the scarce factors zero. With $\delta_j > 0$ for those accepted projects at the upper bounds ($= 1$), this rule obviously does not apply in the present problem. In short, when the upper-bound conditions apply in the optimal solution, the imputed values or shadow prices of the scarce factors (again, in the present problem, the $\lambda_t$) will be less than the values needed to exhaust profits. This difference should occasion no real surprise, because the more conventional dual result is predicated on lower-bound, non-negativity conditions alone; the $x_j$ are free to take on any values from zero on up. Since the dual matrix is simply the transpose of the primal matrix, it should be evident that with no upper limits on the values that the $x_j$ can assume, there are similarly no upper limits on the values that the shadow prices can assume in the optimal solution. The same line of reasoning should make it equally evident that any upper bounds imposed on the $x_j$ in the primal matrix must inevitably result in upper bounds on the optimal shadow prices.

matter. The firm, or its management, can go ahead with them if it finds them to be desirable on other grounds, or it can leave them out altogether.

However, there is another use to which the $\delta_j$ for accepted fractional projects can be put. Before we examine this second use, though, we must take up the question of ranking rejected R & D projects, those from the original, entire set that do not appear in the optimal subset. Offhand, it might seem that for rejected projects, $\delta_j < 0$. Unfortunately, perhaps, this is not so, because being associated with the constraints $x_j \leqslant 1$ in (3), the $\delta_j$ are either positive or zero, in the latter case even for rejected projects. Nevertheless, we can draw upon a closely related concept by reverting to expression (5). It is a feature of dual programs like (4)–(6) that for any particular rejected project $x_j$ (whose $\delta_j = 0$) that $\sum_{t=1}^{T} \lambda_t a_{tj} > c_j$.[8] Let us give to any excess of $\sum_{t=1}^{T} \lambda_t a_{tj}$ over $c_j$ the symbol $\beta_j$. Accordingly, we may define $\beta_j$ as the present value of all future expenditures on each rejected project $x_j$, valued in each period $t$ at the implicit cost, $\lambda_t$, of the corresponding budget constraint, minus the net present value of the rejected project. In this way, $\beta_j$

---

[8] This is simply an application of the duality theorem, alluded to in the preceding footnote, that in a primal problem marked only by non-negativity conditions for the $x_j$, it is necessary for all $x_j$ in the optimal solution that, in most general terms, $\sum_{j=1}^{m} \lambda_j a_{ij} = c_j$ and that, in turn, all $x_j = 0$ for which

$$\sum_{j=m+1}^{n} \lambda_j a_{tj} > c_j \ (m \leq n).$$

is a kind of quasi negative $\delta_j$. And of course, the $\beta_j$ can be used to rank the rejected projects: the higher any particular $\beta_j$, the lower the rank of the rejected project.

To point up the use that can be made of the $\delta_j$ and the $\beta_j$, let us imagine the departure and irreplaceability of the R & D personnel, as often happens. A previously accepted R & D project may, as a result, prove unfeasible. In this event, a fractional project with $\delta_j = 0$ may be expanded to unity or, alternatively, management may choose to bring into the previously accepted set of projects that one of the previously rejected set with the smallest $\beta_j$.

The attractive feature about the ranking of projects on the basis of the $\delta_j$ and the $\beta_j$ is that this ranking is *not* established on a project-by-project basis, as is true of existing R & D project-evaluation formulae. Rather, like the subset(s) of accepted and rejected R & D projects given in the optimal solution to the primal program, the ranking is based on consideration, through the $\lambda_t$, of the relations *among* the various sets of projects as established by the budget constraints.

In conclusion, we would remind the reader that the usefulness of the foregoing linear programming techniques is limited to the choice and evaluation of *applied* research and development projects. As is true of all such techniques, it is senseless to consider their use in choosing among truly basic research projects (as "basic" has been defined in Chapter 1 [9]). The conduct of basic research by business enterprises is essentially an act of faith. Firms may narrow the range of such research projects to general areas of science in which their activities fall. But since, by definition, this kind of research is aimed purely at the generation of new knowledge without specific commercial

[9] See pp. 12.

objectives in view, there is no meaningful way of developing the relevant information embodied in the $c_j$ and $a_{tj}$. And information of this sort is a prerequisite to the use of any formula concerned with the choice and evaluation of R & D projects.

# Index

DANIEL HAMBERG, Professor of Economics at the University of Buffalo, was educated at the University of Pennsylvania. In 1956 and in 1965, he was appointed Fulbright Professor of Economics, first at the Netherlands School of Economics and then at the Bologna Center of the Johns Hopkins School of Advanced Studies. He has served as Consultant to the United States Secretary of Labor, and has frequently participated in Hearings of the Joint Economic Committee of the United States Congress and of other congressional committees. Dr. Hamberg's works include *Business Cycles* (1951), *Economic Growth and Instability* (1956), and *Principles of a Growing Economy* (1961).